RHONDDA
1203 - 2003

THE STORY OF THE TWO VALLEYS

JOHN MAY

Cover Photograph: Bronze Statue - Miner's Family, Llwynypia
commissioned by the Rhondda Civic Society and sculpted by
Robert Thomas. Unveiled in 1993 by George Thomas, Viscount Tonypandy

For Gareth and Rhian
whose roots, like mine, are here.

RHONDDA 1203 - 2003

ISBN 1 871354 09 9

Published by:
Castle Publications, 17 Mill Road, Tongwynlais, Cardiff CF15 7JP
(Tel: 029 2081 1603 • Fax: 029 2081 1049)

Printed by:
Lazy Cat Productions, 6 Western Industrial Estate, Caerphilly CF83 1BQ
(Tel: 029 20 88 11 00 • Fax: 029 20 88 68 75)

CONTENTS

Other publications of Welsh interest by John May:

The Twentieth Century Welsh Quiz Book

The Yearbook of Welsh Dates

Reference Wales

A Chronicle of Welsh Events

The Cardiff Quiz Book

Millennium Cardiff

Cardiff Day By Day

Quiz Rhondda

The Newport City Quiz Book

A Book of Welsh Birthplaces

INTRODUCTION

There has not been a publication for over 40 years, since E. D. Lewis's 1959 publication *The Rhondda Valleys* which has provided a general history of the Rhondda.

In the absence of such an account, this short book is intended to provide the bare bones of the story of the two valleys, a summary of events to fill the gap until a more comprehensive account appears.

The story is essentially a straightforward one of a remote rural backwater - although the popular destination of pilgrims from all over Wales in medieval times - pitched into the stampede of a coal boom with an accompanying population explosion. This was followed by the decline and eventual demise of mining and the painful adjustment of the Rhondda to its new role as a light industry centre, the home of thousands of commuters and a tourist destination but one still bearing the scars of poverty and deprivation.

This simple description does not do justice, of course, to the profound and dynamic changes that occurred in the valleys in such a short span of time, an experience probably unparalleled in any other industrial area in Britain on such an astonishing scale and in such challenging surroundings. A new pioneering 'frontier' society burst into existence working, singing, praying and playing in two languages, and drastically modifying the previously unspoilt environment while placing itself at the cutting edge of political radicalism in Britain.

The format I have adopted of following developments in the two valleys year by year, allows readers to get the feel of the leisurely early years and the frenetic pace of change in the second half of the nineteenth and the early twentieth centuries. Then came the abrupt descent into depression, population exodus and social dislocation from the 1920s followed by the limited recovery of the local economy in the later twentieth century and on into the new millennium.

John May
Tongwynlais, Cardiff
August 2003

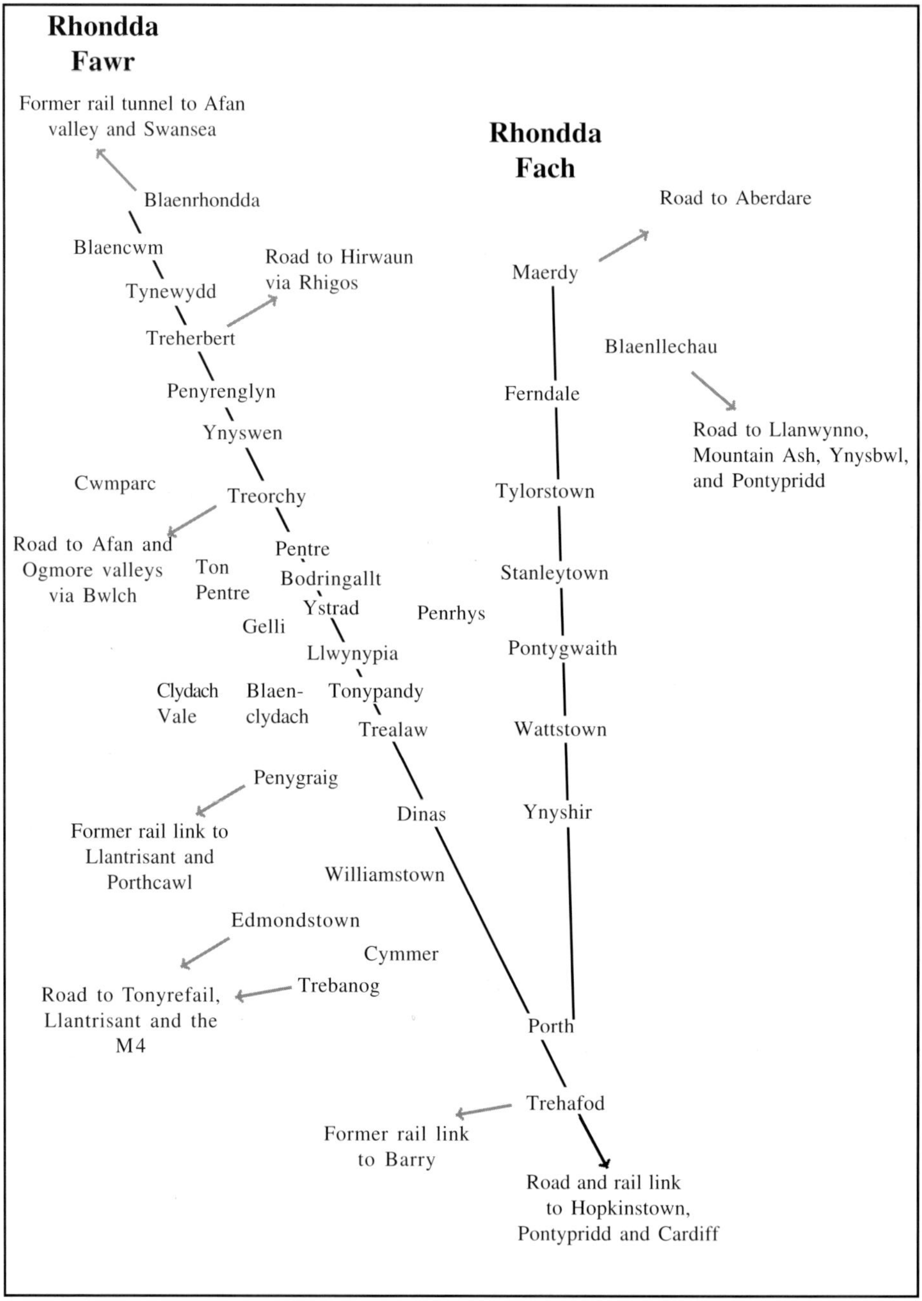

Schematic Map of the Rhondda Valleys

RHONDDA GEOGRAPHY

The two Rhondda valleys in the uplands - the blaenau - of the old county of Glamorgan, are in the centre of the once prolific South Wales coalfield, the most productive in Britain by the early twentieth century responsible for about 20% of the country's output.

In its central position in the coalfield which is roughly saucer shaped - a geological syncline - shallow at the northern and southern rims, the Rhondda has a dozen seams of coal lying beneath it. The most valuable seams of smokeless steam coal are at the greatest depths, while the bituminous coking coal seams are nearer the surface, more easily worked and may even outcrop..

The Rhondda Fawr (Big Rhondda) to the west and the Rhondda Fach (Little Rhondda) to the east and their two rivers meet at Porth. The single valley then extends for a few miles to Pontypridd where the River Rhondda joins the River Taff for its final twelve mile course to Cardiff Bay.

Both valleys contain almost continuous ribbon developments of townships and villages characterised by long rows of terraced housing but the Rhondda Fawr at ten miles is some three miles longer than the Rhondda Fach, is wider and has a greater population density. Only one road links the two valleys before their junction at Porth, that over Penrhys from Ystrad to Tylorstown.

Unlike some neighbouring valleys such as the Cynon, Ebbw, Llynfi, Sirhowy and Taff, there was never an iron industry in the Rhondda. The mining of coal and activities associated with it, particularly coke and brick production, were its main economic base once farming, mainly pastoral, had been marginalised although still continuing to exist among the coal mines and their waste tips.

The steep-sided hills reduce the hours of sunshine and coupled with a high annual rainfall of over 90 inches (2,286 mm.) on the loftiest hills which are some 2,000 feet (600 metres) high, can result in gloomy winters. However, one is never far from miles of moorland walking on these hills with spectacular views as far as the Brecon Beacons to the north and the Bristol Channel to the south.

1. FROM RURAL RETREAT TO STEAM COAL JACKPOT 1203 - 1855

The first mention of any part of the Rhondda (or Glynrhondda in the medieval kingdom of Morgannwg) was in this year with Penrhys named in a document concerning a grant of land to the Llantarnam Abbey of the Cistercian Order of White Monks near Caerleon 20 miles away. The Rhondda was located on the dividing line between the spheres of influence of Llantarnam and the Cistercians' Margam Abbey, but it was the Llantarnam Cistercians who built a monastic cell at Penrhys above the long-venerated holy healing well of St Mary (Ffynnon Fair), which originally may have been a pagan religious site. The Cistercians placed a statue of the Blessed Virgin Mary at Penrhys and provided a hostelry for pilgrims. Penrhys was a major centre for medieval pilgrimages for centuries attracting pilgrims from all over Wales to the Rhondda. 1203

Glynrhondda passed into the hands of the powerful Anglo-Norman family of the Clares with the defeat of the last Welsh ruler of the area, Hywel ap Maredudd, just over a century and a half after the Normans first appeared in South Wales. It is likely that it was Hywel's father, Maredudd ap Caradog, who built the stronghold of Castell Nos at Maerdy in the late twelfth century. 1246

Records of fighting in Glynrhondda during the Welsh uprising against Edward II led by Llywelyn Bren, who was later executed in Cardiff Castle, mention the destruction of four water mills and a fulling mill. 1316

Edward II, fleeing from his wife Isabella and her followers, was captured possibly at or near the Penrhys grange farm of the Llantarnam Cistercians. Taken as a prisoner to Llantrisant Castle and then on to Berkeley Castle in Gloucestershire, he was reputedly brutally murdered there. 1326

The parish of Llantrisant, which then included Glynrhondda, was given to Tewkesbury Abbey, Gloucestershire, by the powerful Marcher Lord, Hugh Despenser. 1348

There is a tradition that this year Owain Glyndŵr attended an eisteddfod at or near Penrhys while campaigning in South Wales during his great rebellion, the Third Welsh War of Independence. 1404

The Glamorgan poet, Gwilym Tew, wrote an awdl about this time in praise of St Mary's Well, then at the height of its popularity, which he visited in search of a cure for his fever. c.1470

About now another Glamorgan poet, Lewis Morgannwg, wrote that it was believed the Virgin of Penrhys brought the dead back to life, restored sight to the blind, made cripples run and gave hearing back to the deaf. c.1530

From Rural Retreat to Steam Coal Jackpot 1203 - 1855

1536 The antiquary John Leland, visiting the Glamorgan uplands, the blaenau, said 'The vale of Glin Rodeney (Glynrhondda) ... is meatly good for Barle (barley) and Otes (oats) but little Whete (wheat).' The existence of a 'Tavern House' at Penrhys for pilgrims is also referred to now some 200 yards from the well. This year's Act of Union between Wales and England placed Glynrhondda in the new county of Glamorgan.

1537 Llantarnam Abbey, to which Penrhys belonged, surrendered to the king, Henry VIII, during his Dissolution of the Monasteries and was given to John Parker of the Royal Stables.

1538 The upheavals of the Protestant Reformation saw the effigy of the Blessed Virgin Mary, Our Lady of Penrhys - one of the most revered sites in Wales - taken from the Rhondda. On the orders of Thomas Cromwell, the king's minister, Sir William Herbert of the dominant South Wales family secretly removed it in September and it was burnt in public at Smithfield, London. It is possible that a few of the Cistercian monks may have carried on their religious life at Penrhys for some years.

1547 Edward VI granted Glynrhondda together with Miskin and Llantrisant to Sir William Herbert.

1579 This was the year the first county maps of Wales (and England) appeared, the work of Christopher Saxton, and Ystradyfodwg, the parish .of which Rhondda was part, is shown - its first known inclusion on a map.

1610 A map of Glamorgan by John Speed showed Ystradyfodwg parish church (dedicated to St.Tyfodwg) but nothing else in the Rhondda except for the two rivers.

1620 A document of this year mentions the existence of a small ironworks at Pontygwaith using charcoal not coal in its furnaces.

1652 The building of Tynewydd House farm at modern Treherbert is dated to this year.

1666 A record from this year mentions rent being paid for a 'cole-mine' in Glynronthey.

1697 The Celtic scholar Edward Lhuyd commented on the surprising longevity of people in the Ystradyfodwg parish, some living over 100 years. At this time the population of the parish was probably about 500, too small and scattered a community to have its own fair or market like Aberdare or Llantrisant.

1735 Ystradyfodwg parish church received its first endowment of money from a Bounty Fund which had been set up by Queen Anne earlier in the century.

1737 The famous Rhondda athlete Guto Nyth-bran (Griffith Morgan) collapsed and died after reputedly running the 12 miles from Newport to Bedwas church in 53 minutes. He was the first in a long line of Rhondda sports heroes.

From Rural Retreat to Steam Coal Jackpot 1203 - 1855

A fulling mill or 'pandy' (for making cloth from wool) was built in mid Rhondda near where the Nant Clydach tributary stream joins the River Rhondda Fawr so giving Tonypandy its name. 1738

The first Nonconformist place of worship in the Rhondda was built at Cymmer by the Independent, Henry Davies. 1743

A Methodist Society was founded at Cymmer 1748

John Henry Evans is recorded as being paid £1 a year as the new chorus master of Ystradyfodwg parish. 1752

A stone bridge was built over the Rhondda Fawr River at Cymmer replacing the type of flimsy wooden structures also found elsewhere in the two valleys, for example, at Pontygwaith, Pontrhondda, Clydach and Ynyswen. 1764

The last of Griffith Jones's circulating schools in the parish of Ystradyfodwg was closed and Howell Harris, leader of the Methodist Revival 'the Great Awakening', preached at Cymmer at the end of the year. In July, the Independent Nonconformist leader Henry Davies was drowned while trying to ford the River Rhondda on horseback. 1766

Large parts of Glynrhondda now passed to the Bute family when the first Marquis of Bute married into the Herbert family. 1776

Parish records show that Ystradyfodwg church bought small quantities of coal from local farmers who could easily remove it from outcrops. 1778

The first six Baptists in the valleys were baptised in the Rhondda Fawr River at Ystrad. 1785

A Baptist chapel, Nebo, Rhondda's second chapel, was founded at Ystrad. 1786

The first attempt to exploit Rhondda coal commercially began with the opening of a level at Gyfeillion, Trehafod, by Dr Richard Griffiths of Llanwynno. 1790

The first Marquis of Bute bought Abergorki and Ystradfechan estates in the Rhondda. 1793

In the first-ever census held in Britain, the population of the parish of Ystradyfodwg - covering a slightly smaller area than the later Rhondda administrative district - was 542. 1801

Benjamin Malkin, who had travelled widely throughout Wales and elsewhere, visited the Rhondda and was impressed by 'Such scenes of untouched nature, as the imagination would find it difficult to surpass'. Malkin commented on 'the solitude of the place' and called the hills at the head of the Rhondda Fawr 'the Alps of Glamorgan'. The first mention of a school in the Rhondda - in the porch of Ystradyfodwg church - is made by Malkin, 1803

From Rural Retreat to Steam Coal Jackpot 1203 - 1855

1804 Newspaper advertisments of this year offered for sale 480 Rhondda oak trees suitable for ship building. - clear evidence of a plentiful supply of local tinber.

1809 Walter Coffin from Bridgend began the first of his commercial mining enterprises in the Rhondda at Dinas with a level. A three-mile-long tramroad was constructed by Dr Richard Griffiths to connect Hafod - where Jeremiah Homfray the Ebbw Vale ironmaster opened a level - with the Glamorganshire Canal which ran the 26 miles from Merthyr Tydfil to Cardiff.

1810 A proposal of this year to build a turnpike road through the Rhondda Fawr came to nothing but the tramroad was extended to Dinas giving it a length of five miles. Local people were allowed to ride in the empty trams on their return journeys after visiting the market at Pontypridd - then called Newbridge - and this practice continued for fifty years.

1811 This year's census showed a population of 973 in Ystradyfodwg and about this year Rhondda's oldest existing stone bridge, Pont Lluest Wen, at Maerdy was built.

1812 The first shaft mine in the Rhondda was sunk at Dinas by Walter Coffin - Dinas Lower Colliery-where the 34 inch Rhondda Number Three Seam of coking coal was reached at a depth of 40 yards.

1813 This year an English traveller, J.G. Wood, visited the Rhondda and wrote '... the English language is scarce ever heard: and a person ignorant of the dialect of the natives would find it very difficult to make his wants known to them, however readily they might be attended to.' Jeremiah Homfray had to abandon his level at Hafod when he became bankrupt this year.

1816 A day school was established at Cwm Saerbren, the later Treherbert, which pupils from neighbouring valleys also attended.

1817 The first known mining fatality in the Rhondda was recorded with the death of Morgan Hopkin in an explosion at the newly opened Abergorki Level, Treorchy.

1820 A medical benefit club was founded at the Star Hotel, Gellidawel, Ystrad, and an account exists from this year of a local weaver who regularly caught six or seven salmon in a morning in the River Rhondda. Anglers were attracted to the Rhondda from nearby valleys whose rivers were already seriously polluted.

1821 This year's census showed a Rhondda population of 988.

1823 Ystradyfodwg parish records mention eight houses built for the poor at Penyrenglyn with money borrowed from the Gellidawel benefit club.

From Rural Retreat to Steam Coal Jackpot 1203 - 1855

The Rhondda estate of Sir John Wood was bought by the second Marquis of Bute adding to his already considerable holdings in the valley. It included land on which the future Treherbert would be built. 1824

A colliery school provided by Walter Coffin was certainly functioning at Dinas now. 1829

During a Welsh religious revival which affected the Rhondda, the first Methodist chapel in the two valleys was established at Dinas. 1830

The first known strike in the Rhondda occurred at Walter Coffin's Dinas Colliery but, opposed by the chapels, it was short-lived and collapsed. This year's census showed a population of 1,047 in the Ystradyfodwg parish. 1831

Walter Coffin opened a second shaft mine at Dinas, the Middle Colliery, as mining activity in the Rhondda slowly increased and the Rhondda Number Three Seam was reached at 84 yards. A new Baptist chapel, Soar, was opened at Penygraig and Samuel Lewis describing a visit to Ystradyfodwg this year wrote: 'The scenery in this neighbourhood is singularly wild and romantic: the mountains, which are very lofty, frequently rise abruptly, and almost perpendicularly from the level ground and present an unbroken face to the summit ... The roads are very indifferent, and frequently prevent tourists from penetrating into these secluded and romantic scenes.' 1832

Just over 50,000 tons of coal from Dinas were transported by tramroad and canal to Cardiff this year by Walter Coffin. 1833

The Calvinistic Methodist chapel at Cymmer was built. 1834

William Crawshay opened Gwaun-yr-eirw Level at Trehafod. 1835

Another English visitor, Thomas Roscoe, felt able to describe the upper Rhondda valleys as a 'wild and mountainous region where Nature seemed to reign in stern and unbroken silence amidst her eternal rocks. Not a human being besides myself appeared to be treading these solitudes nor was there a habitation to be seen'. However, six miners were killed in an October explosion at Dinas. 1836

In October the famous radical Dr William Price, later to pioneer cremation in Britain, addressed a Chartist meeting at Dinas - where another three miners were killed in an explosion this year - and persuaded some of the colliers there to join the disastrous Chartist march on Newport. In November this resulted in the deaths of at least 22 men, none from the Rhondda, when soldiers fired on them. Walter Coffin opened another level now at Brithweunydd, Trealaw, which produced coal for the next forty years. 1839

1840 A Baptist chapel, Libanus, was opened at Cwm Saerbren.

1841 The population was now 1,363 and the Rhondda was affected by another religious revival which persuaded many to become Baptists. This year Walter Coffin was employing 414 men and boys at Dinas making him one of the largest employers in the South Wales coalfield producing some 1,000 tons a week, much of it sold to Ireland. Richard Lewis opened a level at Cymmer now.

1842 The first definite record of a steam engine being used in the Rhondda comes from this year. It was used by Coffin for pumping water at Middle Dinas Colliery. The Mines Act of this year prohibited the employment of women and children underground so the Rhondda escaped the worst excesses involved in using these sources of cheap labour.

1844 On New Year's Day, in the Rhondda's first major mine explosion, 12 men were killed at Dinas Middle Colliery and six more killed at Dinas Fforest Level later. Also in Dinas this year, George Insole from Worcester began his first mining operation in the valleys opening the South Cymmer Level while also at Cymmer Nyth-bran Level was opened.

1845 The first mine at Tonypandy, Gellifaelog Colliery, was opened by Walter Coffin and mining activity now began in the Rhondda Fach at Troedyrhiw Farm between Porth and Ynyshir - the site of the later Aber-Rhondda Colliery, the smaller valley's first pit.

1846 A parish plan of this year showed 63 farms in Ystradyfodwg varying in size from under 40 acres to over 1,000 acres and the parish church was rebuilt now.

1847 The valleys were still so unspoiled as late as this that a further English traveller, C.F. Cliffe, wrote, 'The people of this solitudinous and happy valley are a pastoral race, almost entirely dependent on their flocks and herds for support - the air is aromatic with wild flowers and plants ... a Sabbath stillness reigns.' But Cliffe was the last visitor to make such complimentary comments on the Rhondda, which the 'coal rush' was soon to overwhelm, and it was to be well over a hundred years before the valleys again became a tourist destination.

During the previous 30 years a handful of very small private schools had existed - one in Ystradyfodwg church porch for example, and another at Cwm Saerbren - but by now they had all closed. For some years Sunday schools were to provide the only education available for most Rhondda children. George Insole opened his first shaft mine this year, Cymmer Old Pit.

1848 About now mining began at Clydach Vale with the opening of Perch's Levels but an instance of anti-Irish prejudice occurred when Irish miners in the Lower Rhondda were chased out of the area as far as Pontypridd in November for being prepared to work for lower wages than local miners. Shortly before his death this year, the second Marquis of Bute bought the Cwm Saerbren farm from William Davies whose 600 acres straddled the valley floor in the Upper Rhondda Fawr.

This year Rhondda became connected to Britain's rapidly expanding railway system as 1849
the Cardiff-centered Taff Vale Railway, branching from Pontypridd, reached Ynyshir in March and Dinas in May. The first bituminous or coking coal from the Rhondda Fach, produced at the Aber-Rhondda Colliery, was carried to Cardiff by rail. Ynyshir Colliery (Jones's Navigation), the Rhondda Fach's second colliery,was opened and the first shaft, the Hetty , was sunk at Tŷ Mawr, Trehafod.

Rhondda was affected by the South Wales Cholera Revival in the midst of the century's worst outbreak of the disease which claimed some 3,000 lives in South Wales.

Coedcae Colliery was opened at Trehafod and two miners were killed in a Dinas 1850
explosion. During the first half of the century, no Rhondda pits had been deeper than 100 yards and only bituminous coal had been mined but this was soon to change as steam coal was sought at greater depths.The South Wales coal industry received a boost this year with the abolition of the last tax on coal exports. Surprisingly, as late as this, oxen were still being used for ploughing on some Rhondda farms.

The superior quality of South Wales steam coal was recommended to the 1851
Admiralty in a technical report by Sir Henry de la Beche published this year. It provided an incentive for further exploration of Rhondda's coal reserves. The population had now grown to 1,988 and Llwyncelyn Colliery and Glyn-fach Colliery, both at Porth, were opened together with the Ely Level at Penygraig. Upper Cymmer Colliery was also opened now by George Insole.

The Rhondda coal pioneer, Walter Coffin, was elected Liberal MP for Cardiff 1852
Boroughs (Cardiff plus Cowbridge and Llantrisant), becoming the first Nonconformist MP in Wales. Tŷ Newydd Colliery at Porth, destined to become the scene of a famous rescue operation in 1877, was opened but not until this year did coal mines become subject to the examination of inspectors.

A turning point in Rhondda's mining history was reached this year as the existence 1853
of steam coal - the Four Feet Seam - in the Upper Rhondda was proved at Cwm Saerbren Farm, later the Bute Merthyr Colliery, at a depth of 125 yards by William Clarke acting as agent for the trustees of the Bute estate. They had taken up the challenge of the Taff Vale Railway to find steam coal and won a premium of £500 from the company. After 44 years in Rhondda mining Walter Coffin now left the scene and sold his colliery interests to W.O. Hunt.

From Rural Retreat to Steam Coal Jackpot 1203 - 1855

1854 The wooden bridge over the River Rhondda at Cymmer collapsed during floods drowning a man and at Dinas the first branch of the Oddfellows Friendly Society in the Rhondda was established to provide sickness and death benefits. The first new Anglican church in the valleys, St David's, was opened at Trehafod and there was a 22 week strike at Cymmer over the dismissal of two firemen. Ynysfeio Level, Ynyswen, was opened now.

1855 Salem Baptist chapel in Porth was opened, mining began at Llwynypia with the Tyntyla level, Cymmer New Colliery was opened by James Insole and Treherbert is mentioned for the first time in parish records now, named after the great Welsh local landowning family of the Herberts into which the first Marquis of Bute had married eighty years earlier.

This was an historic year in the valleys' coal mining saga. In late December the first Rhondda steam coal from the Bute Merthyr Colliery was brought in horse carts to Gelligaled, at what was then the end of the Taff Vale Railway, and taken in 38 wagons to Cardiff. There the burgeoning coal export trade had just led to the opening of the town's second dock, the Bute East. The superior quality of the Rhondda coal was quickly realised by customers who soon demanded more.

2. TEMPESTUOUS TIMES OF CHANGE 1856-1899

The first of Rhondda's horrific mine explosions took place at Cymmer New Colliery, Porth, in July when 114 miners were killed of 166 who were underground at the time and all the survivors were severely injured. The mine had only opened the previous year. It was the worst mining disaster in South Wales to date and after this in the Rhondda safety lamps quickly replaced naked flames underground. The coal output of the Rhondda this year was 205,000 tons, still only double that of 20 years earlier and equivalent to a quarter of that of the Cynon Valley, but a level was opened at Bodringallt now and the Taff Vale Railway was extended to Treherbert and also to Ferndale. Another chapel was opened this year, Bethlehem Methodist chapel at Porth. 1856

A four month strike lead to three days of rioting at Treherbert with attacks on English and Irish 'blacklegs' who were driven out of the Rhondda echoing the events of 1848, but the strike ended in a major defeat for the miners. Also in Treherbert an Independent chapel was founded. The Ellis Level at Penygraig was opened together with two levels at Pentre and David Davis leased the mineral rights on 500 acres of land in the still largely untouched Rhondda Fach. 1857

A British (Nonconformist) School was opened at Dinas and was the first such school in the Rhondda. Two levels were opened at Blaencwm, one level at Pentre and pits at Pontygwaith (Cynllwyn Du, later called Ferndale No.8) and Tylacoch, Treorchy. A survey of this year observed that the roads in the area had changed very little since the sixteenth century. 1858

Tyntyla Level at Llwynypia was closed and a pit was sunk at Ynysfeio, Ynyswen. A major religious revival affected the Rhondda this year while parish records show the existence of 26 public houses in Ystradyfodwg. A National (Church) School was opened at Cymmer. As elsewhere in Wales the Nonconformists and the established Anglican Church vied with each other in providing school places in the years before there was a state school system. 1859

A new form of public transport appeared with the introduction on an improved road between Porth and Pontypridd of a horse-drawn bus service while at Treherbert a second British (Nonconformist) school was established in the valleys. Improving transport facilities for the movement of coal, the Ely Valley Railway opened a mineral line between Penygraig and the South Wales Railway at Llantrisant. 1860

With the population now at 3,857 - almost double the 1851 figure - the Taff Vale Railway after operating only a mineral line for 12 years, introduced a passenger service as far as Ystrad but after half a century this was the last year in which passengers were carried in empty horse-drawn trams on their return journeys between Porth and Dinas. The Rhondda's fourth school, a colliery school, was opened at Bodringallt, Ystrad, where an Independent chapel was also opened this year. On Christmas Day an eisteddfod was held in Porth - something new in the Rhondda's cultural life. 1861

Tempestuous Times of Change 1856-1899

1862 A new Rhondda Fach colliery, Ferndale No. 1, began to be worked in the smaller valley which had once been home to just five farming families. This valley in the past had been even more isolated than the Rhondda Fawr with no through road although a small level at Blaenllechau Farm had been worked probably since the 1830s. The Hafod shaft at the Lewis Merthyr Colliery, Trehafod, was sunk now. A National School was opened at Treherbert and the second eisteddfod in the Rhondda was held at Dinas.

1863 At Llwynypia the first two pits of the Glamorgan Colliery were sunk by a Scotsman, Archibald Hood, and some Scottish miners from Ayrshire arrived with him. The first level in Clydach Vale at Blaenclydach was also opened in a part of the two valleys once home to a mere three farming families.

A workhouse was built at Pontypridd for the three parishes of Ystradyfodwg, Llantrisant and Llanwynno which meant that outdoor relief in their own homes for the poor and the destitute of the Rhondda ended and they had to enter the Pontypridd Workhouse. The Taff Vale Railway passenger service was extended to Treherbert and a brickworks was opened at the new Glamorgan Colliery, Llwynypia, using fireclay found close to the coking coal seams, and which by the end of the century was producing 10,000 bricks a day with a mainly female workforce.

1864 Bodringallt Colliery, later called Ferndale No.3, was opened and also became an important brick producer. A second mine, Cwmclydach Colliery, was opened at Clydach Vale, David Davies from Llandinam, Powys, acquired the lease of 8,000 acres at Pentre and Cwmparc and the first major mining combine in the valleys, Powell Duffryn, was created. However, the amount of coal being produced in the Rhondda - half a million tons this year - was still very largely bituminous and not the steam coal on which the Rhondda's reputation came to be based. A two-horse bus service between Treorchy and Treherbert began while another National School was opened in Pentre.

1865 The first temperance society in the two valleys was founded at Ton Pentre and the first coal was produced at Glamorgan Colliery, Llwynypia, while nearby construction of 14 rows of 200 terraced houses, the 'Scotch terraces', began. Another three collieries were sunk at Pentre, Abergorki and at Blaenrhondda. In the latter place the colliery was called the Dunraven - later the Tŷ Draw - named after the major South Wales landowner, the Earl of Dunraven. The intense exploitation of the local coal resources was gaining considerable momentum in this decade.

Tempestuous Times of Change 1856-1899

One of the nineteenth century's four cholera epidemics claimed 34 lives in Ystradyfodwg parish - 17 of them in Treherbert - and led to another revival as people sought solance in religion. David Davies, Llandinam, opened Maindy Colliery, Ton Pentre, where the rich Two Feet Nine Seam was found at 230 yards and the Six Feet Seam at 253 yards. The first coal was produced at the Parc Colliery, Cwmparc, and David Davies leased a further 6,000 acres in the Upper Rhondda where Tynewydd Colliery was sunk at Treherbert. David Davis died and his sons Lewis and David carried on their father's work. The first chapel in the Rhondda Fach, Nazareth Welsh Baptist, was opened at Blaenllechau and a Primitive Methodist chapel was opened in Treherbert. 1866

Another of the valleys' horrendous explosions took place when 178 lives were lost at Ferndale in November in what was to be the Rhondda's worst disaster. As there was no cemetery in the Rhondda Fach at the time and only four small burial grounds in the Rhondda Fawr, many of the victims had to be taken over the mountainside for burial at Llanwynno churchyard. An eisteddfod was held at Treorchy, Trerhondda Welsh Independent chapel was founded at Ferndale - whose original Welsh name of Glynrhedynog had been dropped - while a colliery school was opened for Blaencwm and Dunraven with 154 children attending. The pioneer Rhondda mine owner Walter Coffin died aged 82. 1867

The Rhondda's first brass band was formed at Penyrenglyn in the Upper Rhondda, the valleys' first Co-operative store was opened at Treorchy and Gellifaelog Colliery, Tonypandy's first mine, ceased production. Gas lighting became available for houses as two companies were formed to supply gas in the valleys and St Mary's Church, Treherbert, was built with a grant from the major local landowner, the third Marquis of Bute. 1868

Only two years after the last explosion there, in another tragedy 53 lives were lost at Ferndale Colliery in June. Blaenrhondda Colliery was opened, a new shaft was sunk at Dinas Middle Colliery and the Cory Brothers of Cardiff, John and Richard, now began investing in the Rhondda with the purchase of Pentre Colliery which had opened in 1864 and they soon became one of the Rhondda's biggest mining concerns. The Rhondda's first cymanfa ganu (singing festival) was held at Cymmer Chapel in Porth, the success of the event greatly stimulating the use of the Tonic Solfa system of simple musical notation. 1869

This year another of the increasingly popular eisteddfodau was held at Treherbert and British (Nonconformist) schools were opened at Ton Pentre, Ystrad, Penygraig and Ferndale but with attendance not yet compulsory, only a minority of Rhondda children were receiving schooling.From this year the farmers of the Upper Rhondda were prevented by an Enclosure Act from grazing cattle on Hirwaun Common, something they had been doing for generations. Farming was still an important economic activity in the valleys at this time but was rapidly becoming completely overshadowed by mining. *The Western Mail* of Cardiff went on sale in the area from May founded by the third Marquis of Bute.

1870 This year the Rhondda produced 1.5 million tons of coal and some 30 pits and levels were working including the large Dare Colliery at Cwmparc, opened by David Davies, Llandinam, and Gelli Colliery which was opened by Cory Brothers who established the first of their 80 world-wide coal bunkering depots for Rhondda coal at Suez. Fernhill No.1 and No.2 Collieries were sunk at the top of the Rhondda Fawr by Ebenezer Lewis.

A report prepared for the Privy Council in London was severely critical of the inadequate arrangements for public health in the valleys: 'There is an extreme neglect of all sanitary precautions. There is no due provision for excrement and refuse disposal. Water supply is totally insufficient and liable to pollution.'

The renowned conductor Griffith Rhys Jones (Caradog) moved to Treorchy from Aberdare and made a major contribution to the musical life of the Rhondda over the next decade. Eisteddfodau were held at Ferndale and Treherbert during the year demonstrating the vibrant Welsh cultural life in the valleys.

1871 The population had now reached 23,950, six times as many people in the two valleys as just ten years earlier. A major explosion killed 39 miners at Pentre Colliery in February and a successful three month strike involving some 3,500 miners brought eight collieries to a halt and ended with an increase in wage rates. By now technical improvements in mining engineering allowed the depths of mines to increase from an average of 200 yards to as much as 400 yards at Llwynypia and Dinas. Wooden headframes for winding were now giving way to stronger iron ones with elaborate lattice structures.

A cemetery was opened at Treorchy on land purchased from the third Marquis of Bute and was the first burial ground in the valleys not attached to a church or chapel. There were just four of these small burial grounds - at Ystradyfodwg parish church, at Nebo chapel, Ystrad, and in Treherbert at Carmel and Libanus chapels. At Treherbert, *Last Judgement,* the first oratorio to be performed in the Rhondda, was conducted by Caradog, and St Matthew's Church in Treorchy opened.

1872 Some 30 singers from the Rhondda formed part of the South Wales Choral Union (Y Côr Mawr) conducted by Caradog which won at the Crystal Palace Festival in London this year and the next, so helping to create the image of Wales as 'a land of song'. With eisteddfodau now firmly established in the Rhondda an eisteddfod was held at Blaenllechau while one at Tonypandy became a two day event with the status of a semi-national. Clydach No. 1 Colliery was opened as well as two more pits at Glamorgan (Scotch) Colliery, Llwynypia, as mining activity continued its hectic pace of development but concern about miners' drinking habits led to the first Rhondda branch of the Good Templers temperance society being formed in Ton Pentre.

The *South Wales Daily News* of Cardiff began circulating in the Rhondda from February and the valleys' most important printing and publishing business was opened by Isaac Jones in Treherbert. He was the first to print Tonic Solfa in the Rhondda.

Smarting from their defeat in the 1871 strike, the colliery owners now formed the 1873
Monmouthshire and South Wales Coal Owners' Association, a powerful body of 88 companies which between them produced 75% of South Wales coal. The Association was headed by William Thomas Lewis, later Lord Merthyr. Ferndale No. 4 Pit was opened as was Pendyrus Colliery, an investment by a Londoner, Alfred Tylor, so giving Tylorstown its name. Bethany Baptist chapel in Treherbert was opened now.

A lock-out began at the end of the year which after five months ended in capitulation 1874
by the miners, who had to take a 12.5% cut in wages, and bankruptcy for their union, the Lancashire-based Amalgamated Association of Miners which had only been founded in 1869. Serious disorder took place in Treorchy during a general election campaign, the Riot Act had to be read and subsequently 13 men were gaoled. Cambrian No. 2 Colliery was opened and at Pentre the Rhondda Engine Works were established to supply colliery equipment throughout South Wales. In Treherbert the first rugby club in the Rhondda was founded.

Following the defeat of the miners, the controversial 'sliding scale' method of 1875
payments for miners, linked to the selling price of coal, was introduced in December. It was adjusted every six months at first then every four before ending in 1902 and gave 17 years of comparative industrial peace free from any serious confrontations. During this time the chairman of the sliding scale committee was William Thomas Lewis, the powerful coal owner. Tynybedw Colliery, Ystrad, was opened and was purchased by Cory Brothers the following year. A small number of Rhondda people emigrated to the Welsh colony in Chubut, Patagonia, which had been founded ten years earlier.

1876

The Taff Vale Railway's passenger service in the Rhondda Fach was extended to Ferndale and Mordecai Jones and Wheatley Cobb, both of Brecon, opened Maerdy No. 1 Colliery and Maerdy No. 2 Colliery (later called Locket's Colliery). Tynybedw Colliery (The Swamp) in Pentre was also opened now.

David Davis's son, David, opened the Standard Colliery, Ynyshir and this busy year also saw the opening of No. 6 Pit at the Glamorgan (Scotch) Colliery, Llwynypia. The first performance of *The Messiah* in the Rhondda was given this year.

1877 At Tynewydd Colliery, Porth, in April, five men were drowned and five others trapped by underground flooding and were only rescued after nine tense days in an operation closely followed by the national British press. All of the 22 men involved in the rescue were awarded the Albert Medal - the first time this had been awarded for rescue on land.

After a meeting at Llwynypia, the Cambrian Miners Association was founded and had recruited 14,000 members by 1885, both house-coal and steam-coal miners. William Abraham, to become better known by his bardic name of Mabon, arrived in the Rhondda from Cwmavon to begin organising the miners. Eastern Colliery, Gelli, was opened by David Davies, Llandinam, and with Rhondda coal output now exceeding that of the Cynon Valley Lady Margaret Colliery Treherbert was sunk. The Ystradyfodwg Urban Sanitary Authority was set up to tackle the serious health problems caused by the continuous increase in population in the area and at Maerdy another Rhondda cemetery came into use. In Tonypandy, St Andrew's Church was founded, named after the Scottish patron saint because of the nearby Glamorgan Colliery, Llwynypia, opened by the Scotsman, Archibald Hood. (There was also a Thistle Hotel near the mine). Organised sport was now getting enthusiastic support in the valleys and Blaenrhondda and Penygraig rugby clubs were formed this year while in Porth the Rhondda Glee Society was founded and soon achieved great popularity and success.

1878 Ystradyfodwg School Board was formed which meant that one organisation now had responsibility for all the Rhondda's schools in the year that school attendance became compulsory. A mineral line extension of the Ely Valley Railway was opened to the Cambrian Collieries, Clydach Vale, two of the 34 collieries working in the Rhondda now. Gas street lighting was introduced in the valleys and Salem Baptist chapel in Porth was opened.

1879 In another of the valleys' horrendous explosions 63 miners were killed at Dinas in January and a further important religious revival, led by the Salvation Army, affected the valleys boosting chapel membership. Ystradyfodwg's parish boundaries were extended to include parts of the neighbouring parishes of Llantrisant and Llanwynno. Branches of the Workmen's Emigration Society were founded in the Rhondda, with the support of Mabon, and some miners and their families left for Texas. By now the two Clydach Vale collieries were producing over 1,000 tons of coal daily and the Pandy Pit of the Naval Colliery, Penygraig, began production after reaching steam coal at a depth of 430 yards but Brithweunydd Colliery nearby was closed.

Tempestuous Times of Change 1856-1899

The appalling explosions continued and 101 miners were killed at Penygraig in December at the end of a year in which the Rhondda produced some four million tons of coal. Electricity was first used in mining in the Rhondda now - for surface lighting at Dare Colliery, Cwmparc, and for haulage at the Cambrian Collieries, Clydach Vale. 1880

At this time, despite the critical report of 1870, only 44 per cent of the 9,000 houses in the two valleys had a piped water supply and another report this year pointed out that the Rhondda River was an open sewer and a serious danger to public health.

This year's census showed a Rhondda population of 55,632 as the phenomenal growth of the valleys accelerated. At Trehafod the Bertie Pit of the Lewis Merthyr Colliery was opened while David Davis opened the National No. 1 at Wattstown in the Rhondda Fach. The young 26-year-old David Alfred Thomas, who later founded the giant Cambrian Combine of mines and who was a cousin of William Thomas Lewis the powerful mine owner, was sent to Clydach Vale by his father to learn the colliery trade and he was elected to membership of the Ystradyfodwg Urban Sanitary Authority. 1881

As in other parts of Wales, the pubs in the Rhondda were now closed on Sundays following the passing of the Sunday Closing Act this year - an indication of the power of Nonconformity in Wales at this time. However, this led to a growth of dozens of private workingmen's clubs and institutes to which the legislation did not apply. Many of them became centres for self-education with library shelves full of radical political and economic publications. In Ton Pentre, Jerusalem Welsh Calvanistic Methodist chapel was opened and became known as 'the Methodist Cathedral of the Rhondda', while in Porth the Cymmer Colliery Band was formed, later changing its name to the Lewis Merthyr Band.

Ensuring continuity with Rhondda's ancient centre, the Ystradyfodwg parish church, civic offices were opened at Pentre built of local Pennant sandstone like most of the older houses in the valleys. The quarries which produced this stone can still be seen dotting the hillsides. The Rhondda's coal production this year was 5,300,000 tons. 1882

Explosions at pits in Gelli, Trehafod and Treorchy killed 13 miners and four people died of typhoid at Cymmer in streets where conditions were particularly filthy. Holy Trinity Church at Tylorstown was dedicated this year and the Rhondda Glee Society took first prize at the National Eisteddfod of Wales held in Cardiff. 1883

Another explosion at Penygraig in the Naval Colliery killed 11 men at a time when Rhondda's coal production had expanded to such an extent that 20% of all South Wales coal was coming from the two valleys. Of this year's output of 5.5 1884 million tons - double that produced in the Cynon Valley - a little over one million tons came from the Rhondda Fach. Rhondda was now the undoubted centre of the South Wales coalfield.

A short private steam railway with a 1 in 13 gradient was opened to connect the Cambrian Colliery, Clydach Vale, with the Taff Vale Railway at Tonypandy and replaced an earlier incline opened in 1863 powered by horses.

The renowned Cory Band, then called the Ton Temperance Band, was formed this year and the first higher grade school for vocational education in the valleys - and one of the first in Wales - was opened at Ystrad. There were 71 Dissenting places of worship in the Rhondda compared with three in 1850 as the raising of new chapel buildings kept pace with the sinking of new pits. Penrhys Cemetery came into use now and the new *South Wales Echo* of Cardiff began circulating in the two valleys from October.

1885 The Admiralty decided to use South Wales smokeless steam coal exclusively in Royal Navy vessels, a decision that inevitably stimulated even more mining activity in the Rhondda. But the heart-rending loss of life continued as 81 miners died in an explosion at Maerdy Colliery on Christmas Eve. From this year the Rhondda with an all male electorate of 8,216, became represented in Parliament by its own MP, the first being the Liberal-Labour William Abraham - Mabon - after a Rhondda Liberal Party split on the choice of candidate. Mabon was the first working class MP to be elected in Wales and the Rhondda Labour and Liberal Association was formed to support him financially at a time when MPs were not paid. This year, too, the Treorchy Male Choir was founded and William Evans from Fishguard started a grocery business in Porth, eventually growing to Thomas and Evans's 43 shops in the valleys, a mineral water (pop) factory - its 'Corona' brand name becoming widely familiar - and bakery all employing almost 500 people in the two valleys and many others elsewhere in South Wales.

1886 In this year's general election, Mabon was returned to Parliament unopposed, the first of five occasions on which he was to benefit from lack of opponents, and the Rhondda Fach coal owner David Davis, junior, died.

1887 At the National Colliery, Wattstown, an explosion claimed 39 lives in January and the first hospital in the Rhondda was opened, the Ystradyfodwg Cottage Hospital at Tyntyla, Ystrad, with just four beds for cases of infectious disease. David Davies's Ocean Coal Company was formed this year and the Ely Colliery, Penygraig, destined to become the site of the dispute that was to ignite the Tonypandy Riots 23 years in the future, was opened. The Rhondda now became linked to Newport's Alexandra Docks with the completion of the Pontypridd and Caerphilly Railway.

The first horse-drawn trams came into service between Porth and Pontypridd and 1888
'Mabon's Day', a miners' holiday on the first Monday of every month, was introduced. This was a popular innovation at a time when paid annual holidays were unheard of and it helped to stimulate further sporting and social activities in the valleys but at the same time a Temperance League was founded to combat drunkeness. The house-coal miners broke away from the Cambrian Miners' Association to form their own association while the coke ovens at Glamorgan Colliery, Llwynypia, were now producing 1,400 tons a week of coke of the highest quality.

Cambrian No. 3 Colliery and Ferndale No. 5 Colliery (The Blaenllechau) were opened 1889
and the Taff Vale Railway passenger service was extended to Maerdy at the head of the Rhondda Fach where the track at 900 feet (274 metres) was the highest on the TVR network. On July 18th the first Rhondda coal was shipped out through Davies Llandinam's new dock at Barry, ending the Bute Docks stranglehold of exports at Cardiff. It was linked to the Rhondda by an 18-mile-long railway connection from Trehafod. While digging the Rhondda Tunnel to give the Rhondda a further coastal link, this time with Port Talbot and Swansea, seven workmen were killed in a roof fall. There was no major mining tragedy in the Rhondda this year but 40 men and boys, their ages ranging from 13 to 79, were killed in individual tragedies - all too typical a catalogue of sorrows.

The first elections for the new Glamorgan County Council took place in January with the Rhondda represented on it by 10 councillors and the two valleys' were now to benefit from this year's Welsh Intermediate Education Act allowing ratepayers' public money to be used for secondary education for the first time. Treorchy Male Choir won first prize at the Brecon National Eisteddfod and the Rhondda Glee Society returned from a second tour of the USA.

David Davies, Llandinam, died just one year after his triumphal opening of 1890
Barry Dock. The Rhondda Tunnel was completed and at just under two miles was the seventh longest tunnel in Britain and the second longest in Wales. The Trevor shaft of the Lewis Merthyr Colliery, Trehafod, was sunk and a major rugby trophy came to the Rhondda for the first time when Penygraig beat Llanelli at Penygraig to win the South Wales Challenge Cup while Treorchy Rugby Club was formed now. The building of the Rhondda's largest church, St Peter's in Pentre, was completed, Glenrhondda Silver Band was founded in Treherbert and the intensity of the rivalry between Rhondda's male choirs was shown at a Porth eisteddfod when members of the Rhondda Glee Society physically attacked the winners, Treorchy.

1891 In May the *Glamorgan Free Press* the first newspaper aimed specifically at a Rhondda readership was launched.The census showed that the Rhondda's population was now 88,351, the great majority of its people having been born in Wales - although almost 7,000 were from the west of England - and some 60% were Welsh-speaking. This was the first census to provide information on the Welsh language. But the census showed that the Rhondda had become one of the worst areas in Britain for urban over-crowding with an average of 6.5 people living in each of the two valleys' 13,500 houses. The census also showed that there were 25,744 miners in the valleys and that the Rhondda had some 50,000 men and some 38,000 women, a disparity which may help to explain male domination of Rhondda society.

Rugby clubs were founded at Llwynypia and Ferndale and the Rhondda became represented on the Welsh Rugby Union Match Committee. The first burials took place at Llethrddu Cemetery, Trealaw - Rhondda's fourth cemetery.

1892 The Town Hall, later known as the Theatre Royal, was opened in Tonypandy and a second higher grade school was established, this one at Ferndale where the No. 8 Pit, later called The Tylorstown, was opened reaching the Six Feet Seam at 456 yards. The Nantgwyn Colliery of the Naval Colliery Company was opened and the first lodge of the new Miners' Federation of Great Britain, which campaigned for a minimum wage and was opposed to the sliding scale method of paying miners, was formed at Gelli Colliery. The laying of a new main sewer through the Rhondda with an outfall between Cardiff and Newport was completed, a major contribution to improving public health standards.

1893 There was unrest during a 16 week hauliers' strike which ended in mid August by which time 15,000 Rhondda miners were idle. Soldiers of the Devonshire Regiment were based at Pentre during the dispute caused by the hauliers' opposition to the sliding scale. Maerdy No. 3 Pit was sunk further up the Rhondda Fach from No. 1 and No. 2 but the Dinas Middle Colliery, one of Walter Coffin's earliest shaft mines, was closed.

In a harrowing summer accident, 22 people on a Sunday School excursion from Ystrad through the new Rhondda Tunnel were drowned when their pleasure boat was swamped off Aberavon beach. The first evening class courses in the Rhondda were launched at Ferndale and a pupil teacher training centre was opened at Porth. It was not until this year that Welsh was taught in the valleys' schools although the language was spoken by over a half of the population.

The Rhondda Glee Society competed in the World's Fair Eisteddfod in Chicago, the Parc and Dare Silver Band was founded while the Llwynypia Prize Flute Band was formed soon achieving great success in competitions throughout the British Isles. These developments all added to the Rhondda's growing reputation for musical excellence.

Tempestuous Times of Change 1856-1899

A Catholic pilgrimage to St Mary's Well, Penrhys, took place for the first time since the sixteenth century but was not repeated for many years.

The Parc and Dare Hall was opened in Treorchy while a cottage hospital was founded at Porth. Ystradyfodwg Urban District Council was formed this year in local government reorganisation and absorbed the Ystradyfodwg Urban Sanitary Authority. Like the Glamorgan County Council to which it was subordinate, the new council was firmly under Liberal Party control. The rebuilding of Ystradyfodwg parish church was completed, doubling its size, while following the successful launch of evening classes in the Rhondda Fach the previous year, evening classes were now introduced in Pentre. 1894

In September at Tynybedw Colliery, Pentre, six men died in a shaft accident, the Llwyncelyn Colliery, Porth was closed and at Gelli Colliery a library was opened for the miners. The future Prime Minister, David Lloyd George, gave a number of lectures in the Rhondda in the autumn while campaigning for Welsh Home Rule. 1895

The Treorchy Male Choir sang before Queen Victoria at Windsor Castle, the first Rhondda choir to be so honoured, and subsequently was allowed to use the title 'Royal'. The choir also won first prize at this year's National Eisteddfod at Llanelli.

Yet another dreadful explosion saw 57 miners killed at Tylorstown in January. This made a total of 282 Rhondda miners who had died in 12 explosions in the 18 years since 1879 - a grim price paid for the headlong pace of coal extraction in the valleys. 1896

Ystradyfodwg Urban District Council renamed itself Rhondda Urban District Council, Ystrad Library was opened and the Rhondda Intermediate School - later to become Porth County School - was founded with almost 200 boys and girls enrolled. Also at Porth a passenger rail service began operating to Barry in March and above Maerdy the construction of the Lluest Wen Reservoir was started. Three more Anglican churches were dedicated this year: St Thomas's in Clydach Vale, St George's in Trealaw and St Stephen's in Ystrad. A Royal Commission on Land in Wales reported this year and the document said of the Rhondda that '...the characteristics of Welsh life, its Nonconformist character, and the prevalence of the Welsh type of character, are as marked as in the rural districts of Wales.'

The passionate feelings about rugby union in the valleys was demonstrated when rugby league scouts from Swinton were detected at Llwynypia, frog-marched to the station and put on the next train out. Treorchy Rugby Club was now so prosperous that it could afford to spend £200 on ground improvements - then a very large sum of money. Congregationalists, however, considered football 'demoralising' and objected to children playing it at school.

1897 Tyntyla Hospital was extended to provide ten beds for cases of infectious disease and it was taken over by the Rhondda Urban District Council. The Rhondda population had now climbed to 103,445 with the unhappy distinction of having one of Britain's highest infant mortality rates - 204 deaths per 1,000 live births - and there were still 4,000 houses, the homes of about 25,000 people, not connected to main sewers, about 3 in 10 of the valleys' homes.

Ferndale rugby ground was temporarily closed this year by the Welsh Rugby Union after violence in a game against Mountain Ash.

1898 To widespread dismay and anger, Mabon's Day, the monthly Monday holiday, was ended by the coal owners after a bitter five month strike - 'the strike of strikes' - from April to August during which troops were sent to Pontypridd to stand by in case of trouble. The first soup kitchens in Wales were opened in Treorchy for needy children during the dispute. In the wake of this unsuccessful strike and to create a more effective trade union in place of the seven separate district unions, the South Wales Miners Federation - the Fed - was formed with Mabon as its first president. The following year the Fed became affiliated to the Miners' Federation of Great Britain.

This year it was the turn of the Rhondda Glee Society to sing before Queen Victoria at Windsor Castle. The Treorchy Male Choir, however, was disbanded after 25 of its members formed the Royal Welsh Male Choir and it had abandoned competitions but Ferndale Brass Band was founded and soon achieved considerable success in British competitions.

1899 The first free library in the Rhondda was opened at Tonypandy by local businessmen and a higher grade school was opened in Porth. Three Italian 'Bracchi' cafés had now been opened in the Rhondda, the first one on Pandy Square, Tonypandy - an indication of migration into the South Wales coalfield from surprisingly far afield.

From this year the valleys had their own newspaper when the first issue of the *Rhondda Leader* was launched in December.

The intensive exploitation of the two valleys' coal riches, especially during the previous thirty years, had by the end of the century led to the virtual disappearance of Rhondda's once extensive ancient woodlands, the trees used for pit props, colliery equipment and house building. Ugly black waste tips scarred the valleys' floors and hillsides and salmon and trout, once in plentiful supply, were no longer to be found in the two polluted rivers.

The slow pace of agricultural life, governed by the hours of daylight and by the seasons, had been replaced by round-the-year, round-the-clock work of an altogether different intensity and which was fraught with danger.

Tempestuous Times of Change 1856-1899

Fortunes were being made in the valleys by the coal owners but at an horrendous cost in human life and environmental degradation. The wholesale destruction of Rhondda woodlands made a major contribution to the persistent flooding problems in the two valleys. Run off from the hillsides became much greater with few trees to absorb the rainfall and bind the soil. In addition, subsidence due to mine workings led to the formation of natural dams in the uneven beds of the two rivers contributing to the flooding menace.

Battling against this challenging material scene, chapels and churches arose in profusion to cater for the valleys' spiritual needs and brass bands and choirs were formed to satisfy musical ambitions. Workmen's clubs and institutes were founded while rugby became firmly established as the most popular game.

The Rhondda's well-merited reputation for music, political and trade union radicalism, educational achievements and sporting success was rooted in the later decades of this century.

3. PRODUCTION SOARS, POPULATION PEAKS 1900 - 1924

1900 By now the days of the ownership of mines by individuals or by small partnerships had almost gone and mining in the valleys was dominated by the large public limited companies - Cory Brothers, Naval, Ocean and Powell Duffryn. At the beginning of the century about 150 mineral trains a day , each carrying up to 500 tons of coal, were passing through the Rhondda to the coast although this traffic was seriously disrupted for some weeks in August and September by a major strike on the Taff Vale Railway. In Trehafod the Bertie, Trevor, Hafod and Coedcae pits were merged into an expanded Lewis Merthyr Colliery producing almost one million tons annually but in November four miners were killed in an engine house explosion at the Cambrian Colliery, Clydach Vale. Tests at Woolwich confirmed that coke from Llwynypia was of exceptionally high quality and demand for it consequently increased greatly.

In Pontygwaith the Fernvale Brewery was founded to help slake the thirst of miners and the Rhondda Glee Society sang at the Paris Exhibition. Mabon was victorious again in this year's general election although his opponent, the first Conservative Party candidate to stand in the valleys, received 20 per cent of the vote. By now 35 schools had been opened in the Rhondda.

1901 This year's census showed that the Rhondda had entered the new century with a population totalling 113,735 living in 19,200 houses - 90% of them built with the local Pennant sandstone - and of all males aged over 10 some 69% were employed in mining but Ynyshir Colliery closed now. An increasing number of people born outside Wales were moving to the two valleys although all the previous censuses had shown that the great majority had been born in Wales. This census, for example, showed some 6,000 born in Cardiganshire, and there was an influx of slate quarrymen from Gwynedd during the Penrhyn Quarry lock-out of 2,800 men which began in 1900 and which was to last until 1903. In May, on what had been only a mineral line, a passenger train service from Penygraig was opened and soon became popular for day trips to the seaside at Porthcawl.

1902 The unpopular sliding scale or 'starvation scale' as it had become known, for calculating miners' pay, introduced in 1875, was abolished and replaced by a Conciliation Board on which both sides of the mining industry were represented. On the men's side, some 82% belonged to the South Wales Miners' Federation - by now Britain's largest union. Tyntyla Hospital was extended with accommodation for 52 beds and the Rhondda Urban District Council became responsible for all elementary education in the area under the Education Act of this year.

Production Soars, Population Peaks 1900-1924

The Lyceum Theatre, Pentre, was opened and enthusiasm for orchestral music was shown by the formation of the Rhondda Orchestra. The first symphony concert ever given in the Rhondda, with the Pontypridd Orchestra performing in Pentre, was conducted by Mabon's son-in-law, Percie Smith. These innovations showed valley peoples' musical ambitions and abilities extended beyond choral work and brass bands to include stringed instruments. The Llwynypia Prize Flute Band enhanced the valleys' reputation further by winning the British Championship.

Archibald Hood, the owner of the large Glamorgan (Scotch) Colliery in Llwynypia, died while the horse-drawn tram service between Porth and Pontypridd ended.

This year for the first time in any Rhondda mine, steel arches were used underground 1903
at the Glamorgan Colliery. A major rugby trophy of the time, the South Wales Junior Challenge Cup, was won by Ystrad Stars and Tylorstown Rugby Club was formed.

The Lady Lewis Colliery at Ynyshir was opened and the building of the Llwynypia 1904
Homes, later to become a general hospital, was finished having been started in 1900. The last great religious revival to affect Wales reached the Rhondda which by now had 151 Nonconformist chapels, some of which could seat over 1,000 and with a total capacity of 85,000. Noddfa Baptist chapel in Treorchy could seat 1,450 and was the second largest chapel in Wales. Fred Coombes of Tonypandy won the second professional Powderhall Sprint at Taff Vale Park, Pontypridd, collecting the £100 prize money and becoming the only Rhondda man ever to win this prestigious annual event.

Two more major explosions occurred this year adding to the valleys' grim toll of 1905
mining deaths: at the National Colliery, Wattstown in July 117 miners were killed while in March, 33 men had been killed at the Cambrian Colliery, Clydach Vale. These events caused great anger among miners at a time of growing tension between them and the coal owners.

By January of this year an increase of 3,000 was recorded in Baptist membership in the Rhondda, stimulated by the revival. Even so less than 40% of the population were members of a chapel or church. The religious revival did not deter local people from attending D'Oyly Carte Opera's first Rhondda visit to perform Gilbert and Sullivan. Maerdy Workmen's Institute was opened now and following Welsh Rugby Union investigations of bribery in a match between Treorchy and Aberdare, the Treorchy Rugby Club's committee was suspended, a number of players were banned for life and others banned for short periods.

Production Soars, Population Peaks 1900-1924

1906 The popular local sport of boxing produced a champion this year when Tom Thomas of Penygraig won the British middleweight title in May. In Llwynypia, a statute of the Scottish coal owner Archibald Hood was unveiled by Mabon and at the same time William Walker Hood, Archibald Hood's son, opened the Llwynypia Baths. This was the Rhondda's first indoor swimming pool but mining subsidence was to lead to its closure in the 1920s. Bethesda Independent chapel, Ton Pentre, was opened and the Ynyshir Miners' Hall was also opened now. Tynewydd Colliery, Porth, scene of the dramatic rescue operation in 1877, was closed and dismantled.

The intensity of the competition between local male choirs - like that between local rugby clubs - was made clear when two policemen were required to protect adjudicators at the Workmen's Hall, Ton Pentre, this year. Gambling on choral results was as common as on rugby results, pigeon racing and boxing.

1907 David Alfred Thomas, later Lord Rhondda, began the consolidation of the formidable Cambrian Combine of Collieries - employing over 10,000 miners - by amalgamating with the Glamorgan Colliery Company founded by Archibald Hood. The miners viewed this as a move against them and prepared for a fight.

In the Rhondda Fach, where Ferndale No. 9 Colliery was opened, Ferndale Workmen's Hall was completed at a cost of £12,000 and with seating for 1,000 was one of the most expensive ever built in South Wales. The Llwynypia Prize Flute Band won the World Championship in Belfast, the 17-strong Royal Treorchy Choir returned from a highly successful tour of North America which had lasted almost a year while the 20-strong Rhondda Glee Society departed on a third tour of the USA. The vibrant musical life of the valleys was further enhanced by the formation of the Tonypandy Orchestral Society while the famous hymn tune 'Cwm Rhondda' was composed by John Hughes this year and first heard in public at Hopkinstown.

1908 Electric tram services - the first in the South Wales valleys - were introduced by the Rhondda Tramway Company with 50 tram cars and 300 employees providing a service for the two valleys between Trehafod and Treorchy and Trehafod and Ferndale while the Taff Vale Railway opened a station at Tonypandy - important improvements to the public transport facilities in the valleys. The Cambrian Combine absorbed the Naval Collieries this year and on Penrhys top a 20-bed isolation hospital for smallpox victims was opened. Professional rugby league sides were formed at Mid Rhondda (Tonypandy) and Treherbert but they lasted for only two seasons. In the first-ever rugby league international between Wales and England, Wales were victorious 35-18 at Tonypandy before an estimated crowd of 12,000 and the first-ever Australian rugby league side to tour Britain played Mid Rhondda at Tonypandy beating the locals 20-6.

Regular medical inspection of schoolchildren began in the Rhondda now and the first two women health visitors were appointed to help tackle the acute problem of Rhondda's tragically high infant mortality rate. In Tonypandy the Empire Theatre was opened and also in Tonypandy a branch of the socialist Plebs League was formed at a time when marxist socialism and the theory of class conflict was gaining strong support. But the vigorous religious life of the valleys was maintained with the opening of Moriah Calvinistic Methodist chapel in Wattstown and Beulah Baptist chapel in Treorchy. The Treherbert Workmen's Institute was founded now but Lady Margaret Colliery there was closed and it was not until this year that the first mines rescue station for the South Wales coalfield was established just outside the Rhondda at Aberaman. 1909

The Judge's Hall in Trealaw was opened, paid for by the family of Judge Gwilym Williams of Miskin Manor, and dedicated to his memory. The hall soon became a very popular venue for political meetings, boxing matches, concerts and dances. Llwynypia Prize Flute Band won the Irish Championship at Waterford while the Royal Treorchy Choir embarked on a tour of Australia, New Zealand and South Africa.

This was the year which made the name of Tonypandy familiar throughout Britain when rioting in which 60 shops were damaged broke out, sparked off by a dispute between the Fed and the Cambrian Combine which now absorbed the Fernhill Collieries. The dispute was about payment for working a difficult new seam at Ely Colliery, Penygraig, where seven men had been killed in a shaft accident the previous year and the entire workforce of 880 miners was locked out although the dispute involved only 80 men. Soon 12,000 miners were embroiled in the confrontation between union and owners and some 1,500 police reinforcements were sent to the valleys from Cardiff, Swansea, Bristol and London together with soldiers of the Lancashire Fusiliers, the West Riding Regiment and the 218th Hussars. A Llwynypia man died of severe head injuries sustained during the disturbances. In March, before trouble erupted, the collapse of an old colliery dam in Clydach Vale drowned five children and an adult. This was only the second Welsh mining tragedy to be filmed and shown on cinema screens. 1910

The Anthony Pit at Penygraig began production this year and was the last part of the Naval Colliery to be opened while at Trehafod coke ovens were opened at the Lewis Merthyr Colliery to produce ammonia and tar.

In this politically eventful year, the first socialist councillor, James James of Ystrad, was elected to the Rhondda Urban District Council, while Mabon, now a Labour not Liberal Labour candidate, was returned in the two general elections held this year.

Concern about the peculiarly Welsh disease of tuberculosis (TB), which struck down hundreds of people in the Rhondda each year, led to the Welsh National Memorial Association being founded to begin tackling the problem. By the 1920s, 17 sanitoriums had been built in Wales to treat victims of the disease. Contributing to the safe disposal of waste in the valleys, the destructors' plant at Dinas was opened to incinerate household rubbish.

In Tonypandy the Pavilion skating rink welcomed its first patrons, in the Rhondda Fach the Williamstown Male Choir was formed and providing evidence of a middle class in the area the Rhondda Golf Club was founded at Penrhys, the only 18-hole golf course in the two valleys.

1911 There were further disturbances in March during the continuing Cambrian Combine dispute and 37 policemen were injured in a final outbreak in July soon after the Miners' Federation of Great Britain stopped its weekly £3,000 payments. But the ten month strike, which saw the Rhondda enduring desperate hardships, ended in failure in October and 3,000 of the strikers were not re-employed. That same month the Rhondda Labour Party was formed, challenging the long-held Liberal domination of the two valleys, and the *Rhondda Socialist* newspaper was founded, later changing its name to the *South Wales Worker*.

Because of the industrial unrest, the Rhondda's MP, Mabon, did not attend the investiture of the Prince of Wales at Caernarfon.

In a dreadful train collision at Hopkinstown, 11 people were killed including three moderate Rhondda members of the Fed and they were replaced by three militant miners - John Hopla, Noah Rees and Tom Smith. The census showed a Rhondda population of 152,781 - almost 9,000 born in the west of England - 55.2% Welsh-speaking and living in 29,259 houses, about 20% of them owner-occupied. An average of 5.8 persons lived in each Rhondda house - a slight improvement on the 6.5 of 1891. The mining workforce totalled 41,145 of 55,784 males in employment. Unlike Cardiff or Merthyr Tydfil which had significant Irish populations, less than 1% - 929 - Rhondda inhabitants were Irish-born but over 2,000 were foreign-born. In Tonypandy the Theatre Royal was converted to a cinema and nearby Penygraig Park was opened. The small Glenrhondda Colliery (The Hook and Eye) in Blaencwm was opened but Tynewydd Colliery in Treherbert closed. The socialist Plebs League appointed a full-time organiser in the Rhondda, a clear indication of militant political activity in the valleys.

1912 In Tonypandy *The Miners' Next Step*, a radical syndicalist programme calling for workers' control - not nationalisation - of the mines and for the reorganisation of the Fed, was published. It was the work of the Unofficial Reform Committee and it attracted great attention throughout Britain.

Production Soars, Population Peaks 1900-1924

The Miners' Federation of Great Britain, in which the Fed was the largest section, called Britain's first national coal strike and it quickly led to the passing of the Minimum Wage Act by the Liberal Government. It was the lack of guaranteed earnings that had been the root cause of the Cambrian Combine dispute. For their alleged involvement in the Tonypandy Riots, Will John - a future Rhondda MP - and John Hopla were sentenced to 12 months imprisonment but the sentences were reduced to six months after the intervention of Mabon.

However, Mabon stood down as president of the Fed after 17 years, his authority having been undermined by the new young militant members of the union who challenged compromise, conciliation and collective bargaining and championed class war and confrontation. Blaenclydach drift mine (The Gorky) was opened now.

Ystrad Labour Club and Tynewydd Labour Club were both founded this year, the first ones in the two valleys. On a royal visit to the Rhondda, the Mines Rescue Station at Dinas - just 200 yards from Walter Coffin's first shaft mine of 1812 - was officially opened by King George V. This was the first visit of a reigning monarch to the Rhondda except for the possible one of 1326.

A tunnel had been completed by now for a two-and-a-half-mile pipeline from Llyn Fawr on the Rhigos mountain to Blaenrhondda to supply water to the Rhondda Fawr. The Rhondda tram service was extended to Treherbert and also to Maerdy where Ebenezer Methodist chapel was opened.

The bustling mining industry was at the height of its prosperity with the Rhondda 1913
now one of the most intensively mined areas in the world. There were 48,000 men and boys employed in 55 collieries, 39 in Rhondda Fawr and 16 in Rhondda Fach, and the two valleys produced 9.6 million tons this year, almost one-fifth of the total South Wales output, but there was very little mechanisation and 66 % of this total came from the Cambrian Combine's mines. The Cambrian Colliery itself was the largest in the whole of South Wales employing 4,113 and producing over 3,000 tons daily. Three other collieries in the two valleys employed over 3,000 and a further 18 over 1,000. Llwynypia was the largest mining community in South Wales with over 7,500 miners living there, but at Blaenllechau the Rhondda Fach's only commercial level was closed.

The depths of some mines had now reached 500 to 600 yards, over twice the average depth of 40 years earlier and 12 to 15 times deeper than the Rhondda's first shaft mine of 1812. These greater depths caused serious problems in ventilation, winding and haulage. About 3,500 horses were employed underground for haulage.

Glamorgan County Council devolved responsibility for secondary education in the two valleys to the Rhondda Urban District Council, a highly unusual arrangement and the only one in Wales. In Porth, William Evans, founder of the Thomas and Evans company, built Bronwydd House, the Parc and Dare Hall in Treorchy was considerably extended, Blaenrhondda Workmen's Institute was opened and so was the King's Hall, Pentre, the seventh cinema in the Rhondda. The suffragette campaign to secure votes for women was launched in the valleys now.

1914 As World War One began, a half of the total amount of coal being used by the Royal Navy was from the Rhondda, whose output this year was a record 11.8 million tons, and within eight weeks of the outbreak of war, over 2,000 Rhondda miners had enlisted in the army, a half of them from Cambrian Combine mines.

By now, making an essential contribution to public health, nearly all of the houses in the valleys were connected to main sewers. There was a total of 40 elementary schools in the Rhondda but Pentre higher elementary school became a secondary school while in Tonypandy a higher elementary school was opened. Porth Secondary School, formerly a teachers' training centre, was opened and also in Porth a separate girls' intermediate school was established, Porth County Girls alongside Porth County Boys.

Maerdy No. 4 pit began production at the far end of the Rhondda Fach but the Tonypandy fulling mill, opened in 1738, was closed. Percy Jones of Porth won the world featherweight title in January only to lose it later in the year but the greatest boxer ever produced by the Rhondda, Jimmy Wilde of Pontygwaith, won the European flyweight title. Gelli Park was opened this year adding to the public green spaces in the valleys.

Lord Merthyr (William Thomas Lewis), the man behind the creation of the powerful Monmouthshire and South Wales Coal Owners' Association in 1873, died.

1915 The entire coalfield came out on strike defying wartime anti-strike legislation and succeeded in obtaining wage increases. In the first full year of the war, the Rhondda miners' agent David (Dai) Watts Morgan helped to raise a Welsh labour battalion to serve in France. The volunteers were mainly miners and mining officials. Another Rhondda boxer, Llew Edwards of Porth, won the British and British Empire featherweight titles this year.

1916 The vital role of the coal industry during World War One led to the South Wales coalfield becoming the first in Britain to come under government control, something that encouraged the miners to hope that public ownership of the mines would follow when peace came.

Production Soars, Population Peaks 1900-1924

Union membership now became compulsory for employment in the mines under wartime conditions with 7.6 million tons of coal produced in the Rhondda this year and David Alfred Thomas, head of the Cambrian Combine, became the first - and only - Lord Rhondda. Wartime shortages saw the price of basic foodstuffs increase by 50%, a few almost doubling in price in two years. The unrest that this caused led to the introduction of food rationing in Britain organised by Lord Rhondda.

A major landslide occurred in Pentre in October and it blocked the only road connection to the Upper Rhondda Fawr, underlining the urgent need for an alternative road on the western side of the valley. This was built in the 1920s from Llwynypia to Gelli and then on to Treorchy and Cwmparc.

Jimmy Wilde won the British flyweight title in February and in April went on to take the world title, holding it until 1923 - a record length of time. At Porth the South Wales Bible Institute was founded and Elizabeth Andrews became the first woman to be elected to the executive of the Rhondda Labour Party, a rare instance of a woman in an influential position in the local community.

A Commission on Industrial Unrest in the South Wales Coalfield made the following 1917
controversial statement about the two valleys: 'The Rhondda has an abundance of cinemas and music halls, but not a single theatre. Owing to the absence of municipal centres and centralised institutions, the development of the civic spirit and the sense of social solidarity ... is seriously retarded.' This was not how Rhondda people saw their communities and it caused great resentment.

This year the future miners' leader Arthur Horner together with some other Rhondda miners, crossed to Ireland to join the Irish Citizens' Army in rebellion against British rule there and he was imprisoned for three months for sedition on his return.

The Treorchy Male Choir was re-formed now and Tylacoch pit in Treorchy was reopened after being closed in 1892.

World War One ended with South Wales miners - one third of them in the Rhondda 1918
- at the cutting edge of militant trade unionism in Britain. The growth of the Rhondda's population saw the two valleys being given a second Member of Parliament, with a division into Rhondda East and Rhondda West. In both Rhondda constituencies in this year's general election, the Labour Party candidates, Mabon and Dai Watts Morgan, were returned unopposed. Mabon was now made a Privy Councillor, becoming only the second British trade union leader to be given this honour.

Hundreds of people in the valleys died during the world-wide Spanish 'flu epidemic which broke out this year and the death also occurred of the Cambrian Combine head, Lord Rhondda (D.A. Thomas).

1919 Underlining the growing strength of socialism in the valleys, the Rhondda Urban District Council now came under the control of the Labour Party for the first time. The Unofficial Reform Committee of 1912 merged with the South Wales Socialist Society and joined the new Communist Party the following year championing direct action.

In March Britain's biggest teachers' strike to date occurred in the Rhondda when 1,130 members of the Rhondda Class Teachers' Association came out on a month-long strike in a wage dispute.

The Bute estate began selling its 8,000 acres of land in the valleys, largely concentrated in the Upper Rhondda Fawr while in August the Ocean Coal Company provided entertainment for 2,000 ex-servicemen at Ystradfechan, Treorchy.

1920 Public transport developments saw the introduction of the first motor bus service in the Rhondda from Tonypandy to Clydach Vale, a steep route which electric tramcars had been unable to serve.

Mabon, now 77 and in failing health with his former support gone, stood down as MP for Rhondda West and the ensuing by-election was won by Will John who had served six months in prison for his alleged role in the Tonypandy Riots. This was the first parliamentary election in which Rhondda women had been able to vote.

A new pit, Fernhill No. 5, was opened at the head of the Rhondda Fawr and from a tax on every ton of coal raised, a Miners' Welfare Fund was established to provide indoor and outdoor leisure facilities in the British coalfield.

The Church in Wales became disestablished and separated from the Church of England this year with the Rhondda now divided into ten parishes each with its own church. Although this contrasted sharply with the position just over 50 years earlier when there was only one church in the two valleys, Nonconformity maintained its dominance of the religious life of the Rhondda.

The Rhondda Education Committee gave strong support to the Welsh language by classifying as bilingual six elementary schools - Alaw, Clydach Vale, Maerdy, Treherbert, Treorchy and Ton Pentre.

Production Soars, Population Peaks 1900-1924

A second shaft was sunk at the Glenrhondda Colliery (The Hook and Eye) in Blaencwm but an unsuccessful three month strike occurred in the coalfield after the Lloyd George government angered the miners by handing back the mines to private ownership, an unpopular move which caused a fall of up to 50% in miners' earnings. During this dispute miners stormed the National Colliery in Wattstown and sang the revolutionary 'Red Flag'. 1921

The year's census showed a Rhondda population of 162,717, an 800% increase in fifty years with over 68,000 of this number noted to be Welsh-speaking but only 12.5% of the women in the two valleys were in paid employment.

A new bus service between Cwmparc, Treorchy and Ystrad over Penrhys to Ferndale was introduced and at Blaenrhondda the Rhondda's first War Memorial to the dead of World War One was unveiled.

William Abraham - Mabon - died in May almost 80 years of age. An indisputably major figure for over 40 years in Rhondda's turbulent industrial history, his funeral was one of the most impressive ever seen in the valleys with the streets of Treorchy lined by thousands of silent miners. 1922

William Evans, founder of the Thomas and Evans company, gave the 22 acre Bronwydd Park, Porth, and its fine house to the Rhondda Urban District Council and in Treorchy, Nantdyrus Pit became the very last one to be sunk in the two valleys.

The Rhondda Education Committee dismissed 63 married women teachers as priority was given to male employment in the valleys at this time. In April Wattstown Memorial Park was opened and the Taff Vale Railway was absorbed by the Great Western Railway. Ton Pentre - 'The Bulldogs' - reached the semi-finals of football's Welsh Cup for the first time.

A strike in the United States coalfields allowed a slight recovery in the rapidly falling international demand for South Wales coal - but there were ominous signs of disaster ahead as the fragile prosperity of the valleys became cruelly exposed. Two of the Tŷ Mawr shafts at Trehafod were abandoned now - an indication of the many closures to come. 1923

Over the coming 75 years, hundreds of Rhondda miners were to benefit from stays at the Talygarn Miners' Convalescent Home in the Vale of Glamorgan, given to the men this year by G.T. Clark, a wealthy South Wales businessman. The Rhondda Junior Technical School was founded at Llwynypia and close by the Rhondda Blind Institute was established. In Tonypandy the 1,000 seat Methodist Central Hall was opened replacing an earlier Methodist church.

The small number of people in the Rhondda equipped with the simple radio (wireless) sets of the time, were able to tune in to broadcasts from the new station 5WA in Cardiff from March 1st and this year the Cory Band became the first brass band to perform on radio.

The local boxing hero Jimmy Wilde of Pontygwaith lost his world flyweight title in New York in June.

1924 The French army's occupation of the Ruhr coalfield triggered strikes by German miners leading to a coal shortage which again postponed, briefly, the economic catastrophe about to overwhelm the valleys.

The renowned Pendyrus Male Choir was founded in the Rhondda Fach and Pentwyn Cottage Hospital in Treorchy was opened for victims of colliery accidents. Both the Lewis Merthyr Workmen's Institute in Porth and the Glenrhondda Workmen's Hall and Institute in Blaencwm were opened now with well-stocked libraries like the other valley institutes.

The Rhondda Education Committee abolished fees in the secondary schools at Ferndale, Pentre, Porth and Tonypandy easing the financial burden on parents.

It was in this year that the population of the two valleys is estimated to have reached its peak with 169,000 inhabitants, a figure equivalent to two-thirds of the population of Cardiff at the time.

A Rhondda man, A.J. Cook of Maerdy, became general secretary of the Miners' Federation of Great Britain this year and held the post until 1931.

4. DECLINE, DEPRESSION AND WAR 1925 - 1945

The post-war coal boom was now over and Rhondda began to spiral down into the depths of economic depression, worse here than almost anywhere else in Britain as reliance for employment had been placed overwhelmingly on the one major occupation. Oil was rapidly replacing coal and cheaper sources of coal were becoming available from other countries. In 1913 the Royal Navy had bought 1,750,000 tons of Welsh coal but this year only some 20% of that total. 1925

In a rugby game between Penygraig and Llanelli, which Penygraig won, about 1,000 unemployed miners unable to afford the entrance price to the ground, climbed over the fences and were allowed to watch the game for nothing.

With the recession biting deeper, the General Strike took place in May but was called off after nine days. The miners led by the Rhondda's A.J. Cook, however, maintained their industrial action until November when winter, hunger and debt compelled a return to work on the owners' terms despite Cook's slogan 'Not a penny off the pay, not a minute on the day.' Challenging the Fed, the South Wales Miners' Industrial Union - assumed to have the backing of the mine owners - was launched in the Rhondda at Cwmparc and disturbances there led to a number of men being gaoled at Swansea Assizes the following year. With a weakened bargaining position, the Fed was not as effective as during times of full employment. 1926

One form of assistance brought to the valleys at this time of crisis was in the Quaker Education Settlement at Maes-yr-haf, Trealaw, which provided training and education for unemployed men whose number was rapidly increasing. The Lady Lewis Colliery in Ynyshir, Locket's Colliery in Maerdy and the Bute Merthyr colliery were closed this year and a sporting victim of the recession was Cwmparc Football Club which had to disband. The Rhondda Education Committee decided that Welsh was to be taught in all the secondary schools in the valleys.

Some 250 Rhondda men took part in the first South Wales 'hunger march' to London in November to urge the government - without success - to tackle the area's problems while also in November, a survey estimated that 2,500 Rhondda children were suffering from malnutrition. 1927

The Llwynypia Homes became the Rhondda's first general hospital while Treherbert Cottage Hospital was opened. Morlais Male Choir was founded in Ferndale and in May there was unjustified and unfair criticism of the Maerdy footballer, Dan Lewis, who played in goal for Arsenal when they lost 1-0 to Cardiff City in the FA Cup Final at Wembley.

The Rhondda's transport infrastructure was improved with the opening in February of the impressive Bwlch mountain road connecting the Rhondda with the Afan and Ogmore valleys, a project that had given work to unemployed miners. It was 1928

one of the highest roads in Wales reaching 1,790 feet (546 metres) and was linked with the new road running from Gelli to Cwmparc and Treorchy.

The only National Eisteddfod of Wales ever to take place in the Rhondda was held at Treorchy in the summer with Caradoc Prichard winning the Crown while the Chair was withheld. Among the visitors to the Eisteddfod was the former Prime Minister, David Lloyd George, not a popular figure in the valleys since handing back the mines to private owners seven years before. A successful national rally of the Welsh youth movement, Urdd Gobaith Cymru, was also held at Treorchy while the first official meeting of Plaid Cymru in the Rhondda took place at Ton Pentre.

The Pontypridd Poor Law Board of Guardians - whose responsibilities had covered the Rhondda - was abolished with the repeal of nineteenth century Poor Law legislation. A Community House was established in Trealaw by the Wesleyan Methodists of Tonypandy Central Hall to provide a place where the employed and the unemployed could meet.

In November a rare cyclone struck the valleys and killed a boy in Treherbert and also in November the War Memorial at Porth Square was unveiled. Another sporting casualty of these grim economic days was the Mid Rhondda Football Club, 'The Mush' (Mushrooms), of Tonypandy which was disbanded.

1929 A further spectacular Rhondda mountain road was completed, that over the Rhigos mountain from Treherbert to Hirwaun, its highest point at 1,581 feet (482 metres). It opened in November and again had provided temporary work for unemployed miners. Three weeks after being opened to traffic, it was temporarily closed when torrential rain caused a landslide. On November 11th a record 8.31 inches (211 millimetres) of rain in one day was recorded at the Lluest Wen Reservoir above Maerdy and four hundred people had to be evacuated because of flooding at Gelli, Trehafod and Pontygwaith.

The Lewis Merthyr Colliery was taken over by Powell Duffryn and winding stopped at the Coedcae Pit there. South Wales which had once supplied about one-third of the world's coal exports now provided just 3%. The Rhondda's first pithead baths financed under the Miners' Welfare Fund were opened at the Parc Colliery, Cwmparc. However, the great majority of Rhondda miners still had to wash in tin baths in front of kitchen fires, their preparation one of the many household duties of the valleys' mothers, wives, daughters and sisters.

The Rhondda's first two district nurses were appointed now, a small but significant improvement in the area's health services.

At Maes-yr-haf an Allotment Association was founded for the whole of South Wales to encourage local men to take up growing, fruit vegetables and flowers.

Decline, Depression and War 1925 - 1945

This year it was the turn of a rugby club, Treherbert, the oldest in the two valleys, to disband while by now three Rhondda football clubs, Maerdy, Porth and Ton Pentre had had to withdraw from the Southern League. However, Treorchy Rugby Club won the Glamorgan League this year. In Tonypandy, the Mid Rhondda War Memorial was unveiled and Paul Robeson, the great black American singer and actor, made his first visit to the valleys to sing. He donated the proceeds of a concert in England to a relief fund for Welsh miners.

In February the Maerdy lodge of the Fed, which was affiliated to the Labour Party, 1930
was expelled because of its backing of Arthur Horner who lived in Maerdy and had been the Communist Party candidate for Rhondda East in the 1929 general election. The lodge was not re-admitted to the union until 1934.

A medical report of this year drew attention to the existence of slum houses in the Rhondda where there were 400 basement cellar dwellings. The Hafod No. 2 Pit at the Lewis Merthyr Colliery was now closed.

In the first Three Valleys Festival for the Rhondda, Cynon and Merthyr Valleys 3,000 singers participated maintaining the strong local choral traditions despite the social problems.

During a bitter three week strike involving 150,000 men throughout the South 1931
Wales coalfield in protest at wage reductions following the introduction of a seven hour day, there were disturbances at Maerdy and 29 men and four women were subsequently given gaol sentences. By now Maerdy was regularly being described in the press as 'little Moscow' because of its support for the Communist Party and at Locket's Colliery there, three men died in a shaft accident.

A hunger march to the TUC annual conference in Bristol took place in September and a third of the 100 men on the march were from the Rhondda hoping to press delegates to take action about unemployment. In Trealaw at Maes-yr-haf, Unemployed Men's Clubs started and the idea quickly spread throughout South Wales.

The year's census showed that the two valleys were losing people at a similar rate to the earlier spectacular growth, a 21,000 decline since 1921 with just over a half of those who had left in the 15 to 29 age group. This was the first census to show a decrease in Rhondda population which now stood at 141,346 - a 13.5% fall in ten years. One in three families were on the 'dole', having to seek national assistance through the hated means test of family income.

This was the peak year for unemployment in the two valleys with a record 53% 1932
registered as out of work. This made Rhondda one of the blackest spots in Britain despite the many thousands of mainly young people who were fleeing the valleys to find work, particularly in light industry centres like Birmingham, Coventry,

Dagenham and Slough. Of the 150 members of the Pendyrus Male Choir, some 60 per cent were unemployed at this time.

At the Glamorgan (Scotch) Colliery in Llwynypia 11 miners were killed in a January explosion and in Maerdy the No. 1 Pit ceased production although Locket's Colliery there was reopened. The Rhondda was again represented in the second Hunger March to London during which one of the valleys' miners' leaders, Will Paynter, was arrested.

Hundreds of Rhondda men benefitted from training in a variety of skills at the Salvation Army's 'House of the Trees' at Penrhiwceiber, just outside the Rhondda, and in the Rhondda Fach 13 weeks of temporary work was provided at Penrhys Park for men to excavate a rugby pitch from the hillside for Tylorstown Rugby Club.

During a visit to the Rhondda the Plaid Cymru founder Saunders Lewis described it as 'the worst hell in Europe', and was moved to attempt to organise a decent weekly meal for the unemployed.

This year 790 deaths from tuberculosis, a disease particularly associated with a deficient diet, inadequate clothing, poor general health and bad housing, were recorded in the Rhondda. The death also occurred of A.J. Cook, former general secretary of the Miners' Federation of Great Britain.

1933 The Rhondda East MP and former miners' agent, Dai Watts Morgan, died and the ensuing by-election was won for Labour by William (Bill) Mainwaring, one-time secretary of the Unofficial Reform Committee which had produced *The Miners' Next Step* in 1912. The Communist Party candidate, Arthur Horner, came a close second. He was now editing the new militant fortnightly paper *The South Wales Miner* until it ceased publication in 1935. The Rhondda Labour College was closed this year because of difficulties in financing it.

The Hafod No. 1 Pit at the Lewis Merthyr Colliery in Trehafod and Tynybedew Colliery (The Swamp) in Pentre were closed while in Tylorstown the Welfare Hall was opened. Unemployed men were given 13 weeks of temporary work building a new bridge across the river at Blaenllechau and the Quakers of Maes-yr-haf acquired The Malthouse at Wick on the Glamorganshire coast to provide short holidays for Rhondda people. This year the first Plaid Cymru local council candidate anywhere in South Wales stood in the Rhondda.

1934 Rhondda mines now employed 26,750, a similar number to the total of miners 40 years before in 1891 and Cory Brothers closed Pentre Colliery this year. The third and particularly large Hunger March to London took place to publicise the plight of South Wales miners and in Trehafod the Memorial Institute was opened withcash from the Miners' Welfare Fund. The Fund also gave a £900 grant for the

Our Lady of Penrhys
Erected in 1953 to replace the one removed in 1538
(Photograph by courtesy of the Catholic Archdiocese of Cardiff)

The Naval Colliery, Penygraig, closed in 1958
The site of Penygraig Rugby Club's ground since 1970

Tommy Farr (1914 - 1986), Tonypandy
British and British Empire heavyweight champion 1937

The Pentre-based Cory Band
Rhondda's most consistently successful brass band.
(Photograph by courtesy of the Cory Band)

Treorchy Male Choir
The long-established leading Welsh choir.
(Photograph by courtesy of Treorchy Male Choir)

Maerdy Workmen's Institute to install a complete sound system for films.

In Blaenrhondda the football club was founded and the Wesleyan Methodist chapel in Trehafod was converted to an Unemployment Club. The last tram ran in the Rhondda Fawr in February and the Rhondda Tramway Company was renamed the Rhondda Transport Company. William Evans, founder of the Thomas and Evans grocery chain and of 'Corona' soft drinks, died in February and Jack Jones's popular first novel *Rhondda Roundabout* was published.

The Rhondda became part of a Special Area under the Special Areas Act of the 1935
previous year and a Special Commissioner was appointed to tackle the dire economic situation. A 'stay down' strike occurred at the Dare Colliery, Cwmparc, when 200 men stayed underground for 200 hours over the right to belong to the Fed and not to the so-called 'scab' union, the South Wales Miners' Industrial Union. A mass demonstration by tens of thousands protesting against the 'dole' took place in Tonypandy supported both by religious leaders and by the local Chamber of Commerce.

Ferndale Nos. 2, 4, 6, 7 and 8 Pits were closed leaving a workforce at the collieries of 1,991 compared with 5,654 just 20 years earlier. Standard Colliery, Ynyshir, had also been closed by now. There were still 42 mines in the two valleys, 30 in the Rhondda Fawr and 12 in Rhondda Fach but employing only 24,000 men - half of the number in the valleys' peak year of employment. The expanded Cambrian Combine merged with Powell Duffryn to become the largest coal company in Britain.

The last electric tram in the valleys ran to Maerdy this year and the Outpatients' Department at Llwynypia Hospital opened. The Communist Party launched its own newspaper in the valleys, the *Rhondda Vanguard,* while the Labour Party did likewise with its *Rhondda Clarion.*

In this peak year for cinemas in Wales, there were over a dozen of them in the Rhondda providing brief periods of escapism for many. There were more cinemas per head of the population in South Wales than in any part of Britain: the Parc and Dare Hall in Treorchy could seat 1,100 and the Ferndale Workmen's Hall 1,000. At the National Eisteddfod in Caernarfon, the Pendyrus Male Choir took the first prize.

Rhondda Urban District Council this year pioneered free milk for children in low 1936
income families, undoubtedly helping to avoid widespread malnutrition. The year saw further large demonstrations in Tonypandy, this time against a planned Fascist meeting there which had to be abandoned. However, six men and one woman were gaoled following the gathering. Rhondda men volunteered to fight on the

Republican side in the Spanish Civil War which began this year and of the 32 who joined the International Brigades, seven had lost their lives by 1939 when the war ended. The Rhondda contributed more volunteers than any other British mining area.

At Fernhill Colliery there was a 'stay down' strike by 64 men for a record 292 hours during a wage dispute and Arthur Horner of Maerdy was elected the first Communist president of the Fed. By now there were seven Communist Party members of the Rhondda Urban District Council. The number of miners still employed in the Rhondda numbered just under 20,000 - half of the total just 10 years before - and some of them were working short time.

The government's first effort at doing something for the valleys came with the establishment of the Treforest Trading Estate to the south of the Rhondda, but few jobs were immediately available. The documentary film *Today We Live*, was shot partly in Pentre, Trehafod, Treorchy, Cymmer and Tylorstown. It showed the tragic consequences of mass unemployment and created a considerable impression when shown all over Britain in 1937. The fourth and last Hunger March to London from South Wales took place and 82 Rhondda men participated.

The annual Urdd Gobaith Cymru Goodwill Service was broadcast from Treorchy by the BBC and the valleys' youth movement was helped by grants from the National Council for Social Service to build huts for the use of youth groups at Treorchy and Maerdy. The South Wales Bible Institute founded at Porth in 1916 was closed while a swimming pool was opened at Treherbert in the summer and Ynyshir War Memorial was unveiled in November. The Prince of Wales made a summer visit to the Rhondda and one of his engagements was to open the Recreation Ground at Dinas.

1937 This year 1,030 deaths from tuberculosis (TB) were recorded in the Rhondda, a 30% increase in five years although the disease was declining elsewhere in Britain. The death rate of mothers and infants in the Rhondda was 13.4 per 1,000 compared with an average of 9.4 per 1,000 for England and Wales.

In late August Tommy Farr of Tonypandy, who had won the British and British Empire heavyweight titles in March, failed gallantly on points in New York to add the world title to his successes. A large proportion of the valleys' population tuned into their radios - which a majority of the homes in the Rhondda had by now - in the middle of the night to hear the commentary.

The Miners' Welfare Fund provided a grant for the building of a new hall at Maes-yr-haf, Trealaw, for concerts and plays and it was here this year that the stage version of Jack Jones' novel *Rhondda Roundabout* was first produced. By now one-fifth of all Workers' Educational Association classes in South Wales were being held in the Rhondda but the number of children in Rhondda schools in 1936-1937 had fallen to 25,000 compared with 34,000 in 1928-1929 - a 26% decrease.

The large Glamorgan (Scotch) Colliery in Llwynypia, which had employed 3,960 in 1938
1907 and only 1,135 by 1935 was further run down and the Abergorki Colliery, Treorchy, was closed with Rhondda unemployment at 12,956. To add to the valleys' woes, there was disasterous flooding at Trehafod in October and two people were drowned. The Rhondda population was estimated to be 122,500 this year, a fall of 25% since 1925 and another estimate published now calculated that Rhondda chapels had lost about 70% of their membership between 1921 and 1935.

The number of unemployed in the valleys this year averaged a grim 11,118 but the 1939
first glimmer of hope for alternative employment to mining in the Rhondda came with the opening of three light industry factories - a clothing factory, Alfred Polikoff, at Ynyswen, Flex Fasteners manufacturing zips at Dinas, and Porth Textiles nearby.

The Rhondda Communist Party councillor and novelist, Lewis Jones of Clydach Vale, died of a heart attack in Cardiff after making a series of speeches in the city in support of the Republican side in the Spanish Civil War. The South Wales Miners' Industrial Union, the so-called 'scab' union, was absorbed by the Fed and the South Wales Coal Dust Research Committee was formed to seek ways of reducing dust in mines, a particular hazard in the industry.

By now Rhondda had a greater proportion of children attending secondary schools than anywhere else in Wales but more flooding over several days in July saw Tynewydd, Porth and Trehafod badly affected. The London West End premiere of Jack Jones's *Rhondda Roundabout* took place at the (then) Globe Theatre and the film *Proud Valley* starring Paul Robeson was shot partly on location in the Rhondda.

World war again cast its shadow over the valleys and many thousands of children 1940
and some mothers were evacuated from London and the south-east of England to be accommodated in the Rhondda in private homes. Five community cetres for them were established.

The shortage of labour in the mines, the conscription of men for the forces and the thousands of jobs for both men and women in ordnance factories at Bridgend, Hirwaun and Treforest, banished serious unemployment from the valleys for some years. Cymmer New Colliery, which had employed 2,331 miners in 1914 and Maerdy Nos. 3 and 4 were closed, however, with coal production in the Rhondda now less than four million tons - just 40% of the output in the peak production year of 1913. Important markets for the valleys' coal were lost when the Germans occupied Denmark, Norway, the Netherlands, Belgium and France and Italy entered the war on the German side.

Decline, Depression and War 1925 - 1945

1941 During the nights of February 19th, 20th and 21st, the German blitz on Swansea caused fires whose glare in the sky could be seen from the Rhondda. Then in April it was the Rhondda's turn to experience an air raid: a German plane dropped bombs on Cwmparc, Ystrad and Treorchy causing the deaths of 28 people, including three London evacuees from the same family seeking safety in the valleys. The public library at Ystrad, opened in 1896, was totally destroyed in the raid. In November an accident involving a runaway tram at Blaenclydach Colliery (The Gorky) killed seven miners. Another Rhondda brass band was founded, the Tonypandy Silver Band.

1942 Despite being at the centre of the South Wales coalfield, Rhondda could not evade the rationing of coal introduced this year as the government now assumed full control of the country's mines. The miners hoped that this time, unlike 1916, the mines would not be handed back to private owners.

1943 Because of fuel shortages and the wartime need for power, coal mining had been made a reserved occupation and many Rhondda former miners were released from the forces to return to the pits where 91 % of the South Wales mining workforce now belonged to the Fed. In Treorchy the EMI factory was opened after being transferred from Middlesex, but Treorchy Male Choir was disbanded again. A 'Wings for Victory' campaign in the summer raised £250,000 in the Rhondda for the RAF.

1944 In March Rhondda mines closed during a wage dispute and in June as an alternative to military service, the first conscripted 'Bevin boys' began to be sent down the mines for training because of the labour shortage.

Hundreds of American troops of the US 28th Division were billeted in the valleys for two months from April to May and trained in the area on gruelling mountainside route marches in preparation for the D-day invasion of Normandy in June. A second wave of evacuees arrived now as London and the south-east of England were targetted by German V1 and V2 weapons. In contrast to pre-war figures, unemployment in Pentre was 0.7 %, in Treorchy 1.0 %, in Porth 1.7 % and in Tonypandy 3.7 %. In the fight against TB, mass radiography for chest x-rays became available in the Rhondda and the rest of Wales.

1945 In this year's general election - held after the defeat of Germany but before the surrender of Japan - the Labour Party candidate for Rhondda West, Will John, was returned unopposed. This was the last time this was to happen anywhere in Wales. Plaid Cymru, represented by the writer James Kitchener Davies, contested one of the Rhondda seats for the first time but received just 6.1% of the votes in Rhondda East where Labour's Bill Mainwaring held off the Communist Party challenge of Harry Pollitt by only 972 votes. Glamorgan (Scotch) Colliery in Llwynypia was closed, the Fed was absorbed into the National Union of Mineworkers in January and Ferndale Football Club was founded.

5. THE TWILIGHT OF MINING, THE DAWN OF CHANGE 1946-2003

A worrying statistic in the first post-war year, reflecting a run down in employment in local ordnance factories and the arrival of demobilised men on the labour market, was an unemployment figure of 6,690. 1946

Treorchy Male Choir was re-formed this year, the Ynyshir Band was founded and the Rhondda poet, Rhydwen Williams, won the Crown at the Mountain Ash National Eisteddfod. Rhondda's first intermediate school, Porth County, celebrated its 50th anniversary.

After decades of working toward this end, South Wales miners saw the coal mines taken into public ownership and nationalised, but of the 25 mines in the two valleys taken over by the new National Coal Board, only 15 were actually producing coal and employing just over 13,000 of 110,000 in South Wales, but mining was still by far the biggest employer in the Rhondda. Powell Duffryn had owned 14 of the Rhondda mines and the Ocean eight. The miners published *The Rebirth of the Rhondda* to celebrate the handover and mark the establishment of the welfare state. 1947

From January to March normal life in the valleys was disrupted by blizzards and below freezing temperatures. This was the coldest winter for 60 years and miners volunteered to work on Sundays because of the serious fuel shortage although Blaenclydach Colliery was closed by the NCB.

The National Eisteddfod of Urdd Gobaith Cymru was held in Treorchy, the only time for it to have been hosted in the two valleys. The last Three Valleys Festival for the Rhondda, Cynon and Taff valleys was held and in Mid Rhondda the Cambrian Male Choir was formed. In September about 4,000 Catholics made a pilgrimage to St Mary's Well, Penrhys, pilgrimages subsequently becoming annual events.

Both Maerdy and Maindy Collieries were closed by the NCB but there were now seven light industry enterprises in the Rhondda including two new factories opened this year, one in Treorchy making furniture and another in Llwynypia making springs. Unemployed men were given work removing the huge Ynyscynon tip in Mid Rhondda which had blocked the view across the valley and on the cleared site some of the first prefabricated houses in the two valleys were built. With the nationalisation of the railways British Rail took over responsibility for the valleys' rail services from the Great Western Railway. 1948

At the Bridgend National Eisteddfod, Euros Bowen of Treorchy won the Crown and at the Royal Albert Hall in London, the Cory Band finished second in the Daily Herald National Cup competition. The first Miners' Eisteddfod was held at The Pavilion in Porthcawl and attracted many Rhondda competitors and visitors.

The Twilight of Mining, the Dawn of Change 1946-2003

1949 The National Coal Board reopened Maerdy Colliery with a £5 million investment - the first complete redevelopment of a colliery in the South Wales coalfield - and a similar amount was invested by the NCB in Fernhill Colliery. But South Wales continued to lag behind other coalfields in mechanisation, hard physical labour continuing to be the norm.

The Ealing Studios comedy *A Run For Your Money*, with the Tonypandy actor Donald Houston in a leading role, was shot partly on location in Treorchy and Cwmparc. The Imperial Glee Singers were formed in Porth and the Tylorstown Silver Band was also founded.

1950 Two Welsh schools - bilingual primary schools - were opened, at Ynyswen for the Rhondda Fawr and at Pontygwaith for the Rhondda Fach to help arrest the decline of Welsh in the valleys. Euros Bowen again won the Crown at the national Eisteddfod, held in Caerphilly, while this year's general election saw Plaid Cymru with candidates in both Rhondda constituencies for the first time. A new football club, AFC Porth, was founded at Dinas.

1951 The first census for 20 years showed dramatically how the decline of the coal industry had effected the two valleys: the Rhondda population was 21.2% less than in 1931 with about 30,000 fewer people in the valleys. The population now totalled 111,357, 75% of them in the Rhondda Fawr and the number of Welsh-speakers had dropped to 31,125 compared to 68,519 in 1921.

The steep two-mile-long mineral line from Tonypandy to Clydach Vale opened in 1863 was closed while in November a two-mile-long tunnel linking Maerdy Colliery with Hirwaun was completed. The Rhondda's Will Paynter was elected president of the South Wales Area of the National Union of Mineworkers and held the position until 1959 when he became national president of the NUM.

As part of the Festival of Britain celebrations, a Rhondda Music Week was organised and this became an annual musical event in the valleys.

1952 With the opening of the BBC transmitter at Wenvoe in August, the Rhondda was able to receive its first television pictures but the Miners' Welfare Fund, set up in 1920 to help finance recreational facilities in the coalfields was wound up and the Anthony Pit at Penygraig was closed.

Treorchy Male Choir won first prize at the National Eisteddfod, held in Aberystwyth, their first win for 57 years, and proceeded to take the title for the next five consecutive years.

The Twilight of Mining, the Dawn of Change 1946-2003

In Cardiff, Rhondda miners' lodges and miners' families were represented at the first Miners' Gala held in the city in June. Also in Cardiff, cinemas were opened on Sundays from March and this soon led to a weekly exodus from the Rhondda to see films - an indication of declining chapel influence in the valleys. 1953

In July, at a ceremony attended by the Catholic Archbishop of Cardiff, Michael McGrath, a new statue of the Blessed Virgin Mary, Our Lady of Penrhys, was dedicated replacing the one taken away in 1538 and destroyed at the time of the Protestant Reformation.

Four Rhondda men, Gareth Griffiths, Cliff Morgan, Eddie Thomas - also a member of the successful Treorchy Male Choir - and Rex Willis were in the Cardiff XV which memorably beat the New Zealand All Blacks in November.

Work began on the construction of the Rhondda College of Further Education at Llwynypia on the site of the former Rhondda Junior Technical School. The Parc Colliery at Cwmparc was merged with the adjacent Dare Colliery by the NCB. 1954

Rhondda attained borough status this year and its charter was presented by the Duke of Edinburgh at a ceremony in Gelligaled Park, Ystrad. The new borough's first Freemen were the Labour Party stalwarts Thomas Davies and Mark Harcombe. 1955

The first woman parliamentary candidate to stand in the Rhondda was Annie Powell, who represented the Communist Party in this year's general election, but the veteran Rhondda miners' leader and former Labour MP, Will John, died.

The once mighty Monmouthshire and South Wales Coal Owners' Association, formed in 1873, was wound up now as mining itself was winding down inexorably.

On the site of the future Rhondda Heritage Park, nine miners died in an explosion at the Lewis Merthyr Colliery, Trehafod. Tragedy was still able to strike at the depleted Rhondda coal industry. 1956

A petition for a Parliament for Wales was presented to the House of Commons in April with 240,652 signatures, 32,000 of which had been collected in the Rhondda - 13% of the total although only just over 4% of the population of Wales lived in the Rhondda.

Roy Paul of Gelli was the captain of the Manchester City team which won the FA Cup this year, maintaining the Rhondda tradition of producing fine sportspersons.

The 12 collieries now working in the Rhondda produced 2.38 million tons this year, similar to the output in the 1870s. Three-quarters of the male workforce in the two valleys were still in mining but 5,128 people, over a half of them women, were 1957 employed in light industry factories, mainly in the Rhondda Fawr. This total included 276 disabled men employed in the Rhondda's two Remploy factories and at the Bramber engineering factory, Llwynypia.

1958 Ely Colliery, Penygraig, where the Cambrian Combine dispute of 1910-1911 had started, and Nantgwyn Colliery were closed as was the Naval Colliery there and its former site became the Penygraig Rugby Club ground. Also in Penygraig, the passenger train service from there to Llantrisant ended after 57 years.

The eminent educationist Sir Ben Bowen Thomas of Ystrad began two years in the highly prestigious post of chairman of the United Nations Educational, Scientific and Cultural Organisation (UNESCO) in Paris having been a member of its Executive Board since 1954. Jimmy Murphy of Pentre was manager of the only Welsh football team ever to play in the final stages of the World Cup but Wales lost 1-0 to Brazil in Sweden this summer in the quarter-finals.

Commercial television in South Wales, provided by Television Wales and the West (TWW), began transmitting in January giving Rhondda viewers the choice of two channels.

1959 Ferndale Nos. 1, 3 and 5, Tŷ Draw (Blaenrhondda) and Pentre Collieries were closed while indicating a new political development in the valleys, a Rhondda branch of Plaid Cymru was formed with an 'all English' rule. Will Whitehead, another Rhondda man, took over as president of the South Wales miners from Will Paynter and held the position until 1966.

Jimmy Wilde of Pontygwaith achieved the great distinction this year of becoming the first European to be elected to the American Boxing Hall of Fame.

1960 In early December about 1,000 people had to be evacuated from their homes at Gelli and Trehafod when the River Rhondda again burst its banks and Blaenrhondda was also affected. Tylorstown (Ferndale) No. 9 Colliery was closed and in the May municipal elections, Glyn James of Ferndale became the first Plaid Cymru member of the borough council.

1961 The census revealed a Rhondda population of 100,287 of whom 24.2% were Welsh-speaking. But Rhondda's ageing housing stock was shown to be seriously lacking in modern amenities: only 35% of houses had the combined use of a cold tap, a hot water tap and a mixed bathroom and toilet. There were now only seven mines working in the two valleys, five in the Rhondda Fawr and two in the Rhondda Fach, employing just over 7,000 men.

At the end of the year, pubs in the Rhondda were allowed to open on Sundays for the first time in 80 years following a referendum vote in favour of changing the law, although there were 68 private clubs serving alcohol on Sundays at the time.

The Twilight of Mining, the Dawn of Change 1946-2003

With cinemas also open on Sundays now, it was clear that social habits were changing as organised religion continued losing its influence in an increasingly secularised community.

By now there were some 30 light industry factories in the Rhondda, the largest of them Polikoff's clothing factory at Ynyswen with over 1,500 employees. The Forestry Commission began afforestation of the area with the creation of the Rhondda Forest, a welcome first step in the 'greening' of the valleys.

An outbreak of smallpox occurred affecting the Rhondda and other parts of South 1962
Wales and Penrhys Isolation Hospital was brought into use. Of the 26 people who contracted the disease, six died from it. This was the last major outbreak of smallpox to occur in Britain.

Lewis Merthyr Colliery was merged with the nearby Tŷ Mawr Colliery in Trehafod but now it was the turn of Gelli Colliery to be closed.

Normal life in the valleys was affected by very heavy snow for two months from December and the death occurred of Rhoslyn Davies of Treorchy, the highly regarded assistant orchestral conductor with Sadler's Wells, who was only 33.

Some of the last old nineteenth century wooden cottages in the Rhondda, originally 1963
built for pit sinkers a century before at Tonypandy Square, were demolished to make way for a block of flats so ending a link with the pioneer days of mining in the valleys. Treorchy Male Choir, now enjoying a run of successes at the National Eisteddfod of Wales, looked further afield and toured Switzerland this year.

The passenger train service from Porth to Maerdy along the length of the Rhondda 1964
Fach ended in June as competition from the ever-increasing number of private cars, together with the decline in population, affected rail transport revenues.

Fernhill Colliery at the top of the Rhondda Fawr was linked underground to Tower Colliery, Hirwaun, merging with it two years later and the Rhondda enjoyed two major triumphs at the National Eisteddfod in Swansea. Not only did the Treorchy Male Choir take first prize again but the Crown was won by the Rhondda poet Rhydwen Williams for a second time. However, the Empire Theatre in Tonypandy, opened in 1909 and where many famous performers had appeared, was demolished.

In June at the Cambrian Colliery, Clydach Vale, the last explosion in the Rhondda's 1965
long dreadful catalogue of mining disasters killed 31 men and the colliery was closed the following year. This was also the last mining disaster in Wales. Rhondda unemployment was now creeping up again and this year 14% were out of work. The borough council introduced a 'meals on wheels' service for senior citizens and more of the Rhondda's sub-standard nineteenth century housing, the 'concretes' at Dinas, were demolished.

The Twilight of Mining, the Dawn of Change 1946-2003

The Rhondda produced another world champion now when Alan Evans of Ferndale won the darts World Masters title, becoming its first holder. The major brass band prize at the National Eisteddfod was won by the Mid Rhondda Workmen's Band who edged out three other Rhondda bands, the Cory, the Parc and Dare and the Tylorstown. In Treorchy a new comprehensive school was opened on the site of the former Tylacoch Colliery.

1966 At Penrhys the construction began on a 450 feet high (137 metres) exposed mountaintop site of what was to prove a highly controversial development, an estate eventually having a total of over 1,000 houses and flats with some 4,000 inhabitants and well-publicised social problems.

In addition to closing the Cambrian Colliery in Clydach Vale, the NCB also shut the Glenrhondda Colliery (The Hook and Eye) in Blaencwm and the Parc Colliery. This year it was the turn of another Rhondda choir, the Pendyrus, to win the top male voice choir prize at the National Eisteddfod, held at Aberavon.

1967 In the Rhondda West by-election following the death of Iorweth (Iorrie) Thomas, there was almost a major upset when Plaid Cymru's Vic Davies finished a close second to Labour's Alec Jones, a teacher not a miner like previous Rhondda MPs. The mineral line between Penygraig and the Cambrian Colliery site was closed but the popular Maes-yr-haf Hall in Trealaw was extended. The Treorchy Male Choir triumphed at the National Eisteddfod, held in Bala, making it their eighth win in eleven appearances. Rhondda weather displayed its extreme nature again: on October 30th at Treherbert 100 millimetres of rain (almost four inches) was recorded in one day.

1968 Another public transport victim of the rise in private care ownership and the mining and population decline was the railway link from Blaenrhondda to Swansea. This ended in February with the closure of the 78-year-old Rhondda Tunnel. The National Colliery in Wattstown (The Cwtch) was also closed now.

The last multiple fatal mining accident in the two valleys occurred in October when three men were killed in a roof fall at Maerdy Colliery. Maintaining the lively musical traditions of the valleys, a Rhondda Symphony Orchestra was formed and replacing TWW, HTV began providing commercial television in the valleys.

1969 Three Rhondda veterans died this year: JimmyWilde, the former world flyweight boxing champion; Arthur Horner, the first Communist president of the Fed; and Emrys Hughes, the long-serving Labour MP for South Ayrshire, Scotland.

By this time the construction of the Penrhys Estate had been completed and hundreds of trees were planted to provide windbreaks but soon became victims of sheep, gales and vandals. The Aberfan tragedy of 1966 in the neighbouring Taff

Valley led to a major land reclamation programme in Wales and Rhondda colliery and waste tip sites began to be cleared.

As a precaution, just over three years after the appalling Aberfan disaster, a mass evacuation took place in the Rhondda Fach in January on the instructions of George Thomas, Secretary of State for Wales from 1968, after a crack was detected in the wall of the Lluest Wen Reservoir above Maerdy. Gelli in the Rhondda Fawr was again affected by flooding. 1970

In this year's general election, Elfed Davies, Labour MP for Rhondda East, was one of the last two MPs in Wales to be sponsored by the National Union of Mineworkers - soon there would be none of the 13 there once were.

At Llwynypia the first World and second European archery championships were held at Glyn Cornel, while the Gaiety Cinema, Treherbert, was demolished and Fernvale Brewery, Pontygwaith, closed after 70 years. The Cory Band won the Coal Industry Championships and retained the title for the next two years. In December Graig Park, the new Penygraig rugby ground, was officially opened on the site of the former Naval Colliery and the death occurrred of Arthur Duggan, the highly respected former conductor of the Pendyrus Male Choir.

This year's census showed the Rhondda population was continuing to fall and now totalled 88,816 of whom 13.6% were Welsh-speaking. Almost 10,000 people living in the Rhondda were now commuting to jobs outside the two valleys, although light industry manufacturing was providing significant employment - for 750 at the EMI plant in Treorchy, for example. 1971

The death occurred of William (Bill) Mainwaring, former Labour MP for Rhondda East and one of the authors of the famous document of 1912 *The Miners' Next Step*, published in the aftermath of the Tonypandy Riots. The Quakers relinquished control of their Maes-yr-haf Settlement in Trealaw in November and it was taken over by Rhondda Borough Council to become a community centre.

The first national coal strike since 1926 was called by the NUM on January 9th and by mid-February the country's industry was on a three day working week because of the winter fuel shortage. The strike ended on February 28th with a settlement of the miners' pay demands. 1972

Another sporting success for the Rhondda came in the summer when Mal Evans of Ton Pentre won the bowls world singles outdoor title in Worthing.

The first-ever Japanese rugby team to tour Europe played its opening game at Penygraig on the new club ground there. The death occurred this year of a Rhondda Welsh rugby star from the early years of the century - Willie Llywellyn, a member 1973 of the Wales team which memorably beat the first New Zealand All Blacks at Cardiff in 1905.

The former separate Porth County boys' and girls' schools were merged in a comprehensive school.

1974 Another national coal strike in support of a wage claim was called on February 9th after an overtime ban begun in the previous November and, like the 1972 strike, this soon led to a three day working week again. A general election over the issue was called by the Conservative government of Edward Heath and it was won by Labour - the first of two general election successes for the party this year. Because of the continuing decline in population, the Rhondda's representation in Parliament was now reduced to one MP after 56 years with two.

In the second of the year's elections, Alec Jones was returned as Labour MP with the largest majority ever recorded in Wales, 38,654 and in major local government reform, Rhondda became part of the new county of Mid Glamorgan.

John Davies of Llwynypia won a silver medal in the steeplechase at the Commonwealth Games in New Zealand while the Cory Band won the British Championship, the first band from Wales to do so.

1975 The open air swimming pool in Gelligaled Park, Ystrad, opened in the mid-1930s with funding from the Miners' Welfare Fund, was demolished as the impressive £1 million Rhondda Sports Centre with an indoor pool was opened in the park and Alan Evans of Ferndale won the darts British Open Championship.

In this year's referendum, the Rhondda was part of Mid Glamorgan which voted by 147,348 votes to 111,672 to remain in the European Community.

1976 Sir Stanley Baker, the Ferndale-born stage and screen actor and film producer, died in Malaga, Spain, soon after completing work on the BBC TV production of *How Green Was My Valley*, which also starred another Rhondda actor, Ray Smith of Trealaw.

George Thomas was elected Speaker of the House of Commons, becoming only the fifth Welshman to have held this office, while Clive Thomas of Treorchy this year became one of only three Welshmen to have controlled an FA Cup Final.

Blaenrhondda was designated a conservation area because of the surviving nineteenth century housing there but in September at Trehafod a slurry landslide and rockfall engulfed 15 houses, injuring one person.

1977 The death occurred of the eminent educationist Sir Ben Bowen Thomas of Ystrad, former Warden of Coleg Harlech, Gwynedd, and one-time head of UNESCO in Paris.

The Twilight of Mining, the Dawn of Change 1946-2003

Another milestone in Rhondda's industrial history was passed as Fernhill Colliery, the last mine in the Upper Rhondda Fawr, was closed by the NCB, and the well-known novelist and short story writer, Rhys Davies of Blaenclydach, died. In Penygraig a new comprehensive school replacing the one in Tonypandy was opened on the reclaimed Nantgwyn Colliery site. 1978

In the St David's Day referendum on establishing a Welsh Assembly, Rhondda was part of Mid Glamorgan which voted by 184,196 to 46,747 against it. 1979

The Rhondda secured itself a unique position in British political history this year when Annie Powell became mayor of the borough - the first and only Communist Party member ever to become a mayor anywhere in Britain. At the end of the year both Blaencwm and Trehafod were affected by serious flooding.

The first Rhondda ten mile 'fun run' for charity was held in the summer and attracted hundreds of participants, while the Cory Band brought more musical glory to the Rhondda by winning the European Championship. 1980

This year's census showed the Rhondda's population to be down to 81,089 of whom just 9.4% were now Welsh-speaking. This total figure was very similar to the two valleys' population a hundred years earlier. 1981

Just before Christmas, the rural dean of the Rhondda, Kenneth Gillingham, resigned in protest following the ordination at Llandaff Cathedral of Mrs Iris Thomas of Maerdy as the first woman deacon. The Rhondda novelist, dramatist and humourist Cymmer-born Gwyn Thomas died.

The Cory Band won the British Championship again eight years after first winning the title. In January blizzards and continuous sub-zero temperatures played havoc with normal life in the valleys for weeks. 1982

After 30 years the annual South Wales Miners' Gala in Cardiff ended and the Lewis Merthyr Colliery at Trehafod, now the site of the Rhondda Heritage Park, was closed leaving Maerdy Colliery as Rhondda's sole surviving coal mine employing just 900 men. A vigorous national campaign had been organised to keep the mine open but proved futile. 1983

Rhondda Community Arts was set up to encourage local people - including the disabled - to become involved in the valleys' social, cultural and educational life. This was part of a wide-ranging ambitious programme to bring people into decision-making processes to help shape their society directly.

Alec Jones, the Rhondda's MP, died and for the rest of the century Rhondda was represented in Parliament by Labour's Allan Rogers who won this year's general election. George Thomas stepped down from his position as Speaker of the House of Commons, was made an hereditary peer and took the title of Viscount Tonypandy. The Cory Band again won the British Championship.

A flood prevention scheme at Gelli was completed and Soar Baptist chapel at Penygraig, founded 150 years earlier, was converted to become the Ffrwdamos Community Centre.

1984 The year saw the beginning of the last coal dispute to affect the communities of South Wales when Maerdy Colliery was one of the area's remaining 28 pits with a total 20,000 workforce which joined the 12-month-long national miners' strike against pit closures.

The Cory Band won the British Championship for the third consecutive year and the death occurred of the former Rhondda and national miners' leader and Spanish Civil War veteran, Will Paynter.

1985 The miners' strike ended in defeat at the hands of Margaret Thatcher's Conservative government but support for the action had remained strong in the Rhondda with the formation of miners' support groups in which local women played a particularly active role. The dispute proved to be one of the most bitter ever to effect the South Wales mining communities

At Maerdy, the Archbishop of Wales, Derrick Childs, unveiled a plaque in memory of the 81 miners who died in the 1885 explosion there - it was a poignant link between the heyday of Rhondda mining and the vanishing mining present.

Another Rhondda flood protection scheme was completed, this time at Trehafod, and Glyn James of Ferndale became the first Plaid Cymru mayor of the Rhondda.

On the site of the former Cambrian Colliery, Clydach Vale, work began on a £2.5 million land reclamation scheme.

1986 Almost the final act in Rhondda's dramatic coal mining history came on June 30th when the last coal was raised at the last mine, Maerdy Colliery, but the mine remained open with just over 80 men employed and linked to Tower Colliery, Hirwaun.

In February the first length of the much-needed Rhondda-M4 link road was opened between Williamstown and Coedely but the valleys said farewell to some of its notable figures who died this year: Tommy Farr, the heavyweight boxing champion, Annie Powell, Rhondda's former Communist mayor, and Mansel Thomas the composer and conductor from Pontygwaith.

The Treorchy Male Choir sang at the Sydney Opera House becoming the first Welsh choir to do so.

At Llwynypia the building of an extension to the Rhondda College was finished and the construction of a new St John's Church near the site of the old Ystradyfodwg parish church was completed. The borough council, looking to the future, held a trade fair in October to attract new businesses and encourage tourism but an attempt to create a western-style theme park on the former Fernhill Colliery site in Blaenrhondda ended in failure this year. With privatisation of the mines planned, the National Coal Board became British Coal. 1987

In October the £6.7 million four-mile-long Mid Rhondda access road, including the Penygraig-Tonypandy bypass, was completed putting Mid Rhondda only some 20 minutes away from the M4 - a major improvement in the valleys' transport infrastructure. 1988

The Rhondda was not forgetting its past and two more mining memorials were unveiled now one at Ferndale to the victims of the 1867 and 1869 disasters and another at Cymmer in tribute to the 114 miners killed in the New Cymmer Colliery explosion of 1856.

Another eminent Rhondda man, Euros Bowen of Treorchy, winner of the Crown at both the 1948 and 1950 National Eisteddfodau, died this year while at Cymmer a Welsh-language comprehensive school was opened with an initial 85 pupils - a clear indication of a revival of interest in the language.

Rhondda was now turning its attention towards a new industry, tourism, and the first stage of the Rhondda Heritage Park was opened in July on the site of the old Lewis Merthyr Colliery in Trehafod. This was partly financed by the Valleys Initiative launched at Llwynypia in 1988 by Peter Walker, the Conservative Secretary of State for Wales. 1989

Rhondda's mining history ended with the closure of the valleys' last mine, Maerdy Colliery, on December 21st, exactly 145 years to the day after the first Rhondda steam coal had been sent to Cardiff for shipment and 200 years after Dr Richard Griffiths began the commercial working of bituminous coal at Trehafod. Since then some 100 mines had been worked in the Rhondda and the final closure received the attention of the national British media as the long reign of King Coal in these most famous of mining valleys was terminated. The site was subsequently cleared for light industry factory units to be built. 1990

Maerdy Community Centre was opened this year in the former police station there and Pentwyn Cottage Hospital in Treorchy was closed to become a nursing home.

This year's census revealed that the population of the Rhondda had dropped to 78,344 - 3.8% less than in 1981. Of this total 93.8% had been born in Wales but now only 8.2% were Welsh-speaking. The total population was under a half of that at 1991 the peak in 1924 when the estimated population was 169,000. A striking feature of housing in the Rhondda was that 78% of the homes were owner-occupied, one of the highest figures in the UK. The census also showed that 45% of households in the Rhondda did not have a car which meant a heavy dependence by many people, especially the elderly and disabled, on public transport particularly buses.

The Rhondda's first new hospital for over 60 years, the 50-bed Ysbyty George Thomas in Treorchy, was opened - a beneficiary of the 1988 Valleys Initiative as was the Parc and Dare Hall, also in Treorchy, which received about £500,000 . The 'Black Gold' exhibition at the Heritage Park was opened to tell the story of Rhondda's mining past to visitors.

The deaths occurred of two well-known Rhondda actors, Donald Houston of Tonypandy and Ray Smith of Trealaw and the highly respected conductor of the Treorchy Male Choir, John Haydn Davies of Blaencwm, also died now.

1992 The Rhondda established its own tourist board this year, hopeful of taking advantage of publicity for the South Wales valleys gained from the Ebbw Vale Garden Festival of Wales. The Rhigos mountain road between Treherbert and Hirwaun was closed for three months from February because of subsidence while in December, following very heavy rainfall, a number of houses were affected by landslides at Blaenllechau, Tylorstown and Pontygwaith. Rhondda weather was still continuing to pose major problems in the community.

A memorial garden was opened on the reclaimed site of the Cambrian Colliery, Clydach Vale, dedicated to the victims of the 1905 and 1965 explosions there.

1993 At Llwynypia, on the site of the former Glamorgan (Scotch) Colliery, the statue of a mining family was unveiled by George Thomas, Viscount Tonypandy, to be a permanent reminder of the people who had made the name of the Rhondda synonymous with Welsh coal. (See the cover photograph).

This was the year that the Conservative government's second five-year Valleys Initiative was launched to tackle the area's social and economic problems, although the move was received with some scepticism locally.

Treorchy Rugby Club won the Welsh Rugby Union's Division Three championship earning promotion to Division Two.

1994 There was flooding again in late December which interrupted train services to Treherbert and at Llwynypia a new magistrates' court building was opened on the site of the former Glamorgan Colliery's stables.

An 'Underground Experience' was added to the Rhondda Heritage Park tourist attraction at Trehafod although the site was still not as ambitious as originally planned. The Tower Colliery at Hirwaun was bought by its 250 workforce which included some Rhondda miners working in what was the last shaft mine in Wales.

Treherbert open air baths were demolished and replaced by an indoor pool and the name of Mel Hopkins, the football star from Pentre, was added to the Welsh Sports Hall of Fame at the Museum of Welsh Life at St Fagans. Three other Rhondda sports personalities already there were Cliff Jones and Cliff Morgan, both Welsh rugby internationals, and the boxer Jimmy Wilde.

Treorchy Rugby Club continued its winning ways by topping the Division Two table, getting promotion to Division One and encounters with the major club names of Welsh rugby. The problems of professional rugby union were yet to emerge.

A vigorous campaign called RANT (Residents Against Nant-y-gwyddon Tip), 1995
was launched now to stop tipping at Rhondda's only landfill site at Nant-y-gwyddon, Gelli, as local people considered the site to be a risk to public health. They showed they were not prepared to accept meekly decisions adversely affecting their community. Another local problem began to be tackled when the borough council started to demolish some of the houses on the troubled and controversial Penrhys Estate to reduce the number of homes from the original 1,000 to about 700.

Ferndale Workmen's Hall, opened in 1907, was demolished, Ton Pentre became the first Welsh football club to qualify for the European InterToto competition by finishing third in the League of Wales and Richie Burnett of Cwmparc won the darts world title. In Tylorstown, the Rhondda Fach Sports Centre was officially opened in April on reclaimed colliery land.

Musically, Rhondda was still striking the right notes as by the time the National Youth Orchestra of Wales celebrated its half-centenary now, some 30 young people from the Rhondda had played in it. In education, the Rhondda College was merged with Pontypridd College and later became a campus of Coleg Morgannwg.

Major local government reorganisation saw the Rhondda lose its proud local 1996
government independence and become absorbed into the new all-purpose borough of Rhondda Cynon Taff. However, the headquarters buildings of the new unitary authority were at Clydach Vale on the site of the former Cambrian Colliery, now called Cambrian Park.

In the Rhondda Fach, local initiative led to the formation of the Blaenllechau Enterprise for Lifelong Learning (BELL) as a regeneration scheme to create a focus for communal activity. The BELL centre in the valley soon became linked to the University of Glamorgan as part of its Community Unit of the Valleys.

1997 With the privatisation of British Rail this year, the Cardiff Railway Company - later Wales and Borders trains - took over the passenger train service in the valleys which had begun in 1861.

In the devolution referendum on the establishment of a National Assembly for Wales, Rhondda was part of the electorate which voted in favour by 51,201 'Yes' votes to 36,362 'No' votes. In this year's general election - won by Labour - Leane Wood of Plaid Cymru became only the second woman ever to stand as a parliamentary candidate in the Rhondda while the campaign against the Nant-y-gwyddon landfill site at Gelli succeeded in getting the tipping suspended.
Two Rhondda writers with considerable reputations died this year: Ron Berry from Blaencwm, noted for the gritty, unsentimental realism of his novels and short stories, and Rhydwen Williams of Ystrad, poet and novelist and winner of the Crown at the National Eisteddfodau of 1946 and 1964.

1998 In another major public transport change, the Scottish-based bus company, Stagecoach, took over the 90-year-old Rhondda Transport Company while in changes to the Territorial Army, the Pentre TA centre was downgraded to the status of a cadet establishment.

The deaths occured of George Thomas, Viscount Tonypandy, former Secretary of State for Wales and Speaker of the House of Commons, and also of Geraint Jones, the noted conductor and organist from Porth. In Llwynypia Hospital the death occurred of Dorothy Squires, the popular Welsh singing star, who had been living in retirement in Trebanog.

The great American singer and actor Paul Robeson, who had died in 1976 and who was held in great esteem and affection in South Wales, was made an Honorary Welshman with an exhibition at the Parc and Dare Hall, Treorchy, opened in his honour.

The former Miners' Convalescent Home at Talygarn in the Vale of Glamorgan was closed now, many Rhondda miners having benefitted from its care over the years since it opened in 1923.

1999 The century ended with political sensations in the Rhondda. In the first elections for the new National Assembly for Wales, the Plaid Cymru candidate Geraint Davies, beat Wayne David, the former leader of the Labour group in the European Parliament while the new Rhondda Cynon Taff Borough Council came under Plaid Cymru control with 17 of the authority's ruling 42 Plaid Cymru councillors returned from the Rhondda's 15 wards.

More notable Rhondda people died this year: Alan Evans from Ferndale, the first World Darts Champion in 1965, the sculptor Robert Thomas of Cwmparc and the painter Ernest Zobole of Ystrad, both members of the 'Rhondda Group' of artists.

The Twilight of Mining, the Dawn of Change 1946-2003

In May at the Rhondda Heritage Park, Trehafod, a memorial to all the miners of the South Wales coalfield who died because of accidents, injuries and dust disease was unveiled. Well over 1,000 miners had been killed in accidents, mainly explosions, in the Rhondda itself while the lives of many thousands of others had been shortened tragically as a result of their work. The new millennium thus began with a tribute to the past coupled with hopes for a post-industrial future free from the dangers of earlier times but bringing its own challenges, opportunites and rewards. 2000

One hopeful sign of a more confident new Rhondda emerging was the reopening of the former Thomas and Evans 'Corona' mineral water factory in Porth as The Pop Factory music centre with recording studios. Tom Jones gave the venture his support by attending the official opening in September together with Kelly Jones of the Stereophonics and Cerys Matthews.

A major figure in the musical life of the Rhondda died at the end of the year - Glynne Jones, the long-serving conductor of the Pendyrus Male Choir. The death also occurred of the Ystrad-born Cardiff rugby star, Rex Willis, Welsh international and British Lion. The Cory Band maintained its high musical profile by winning both the British Open and the National Championship, a highly prestigious double.

The 'greening' of the valleys continued with the opening of the Maerdy Community Woodland near the Maerdy-Aberdare road.

The century's first census showed a further drop in population but not as marked as in recent censuses - under 2,000 - and a small but significant increase in the number of Welsh-speakers was recorded, a trend common to many parts of Wales. 2001

Plaid Cymru's 1999 election successes in the Rhondda were not repeated in this year's general election. It was won by Labour's Chris Bryant with the second largest majority in all of the 40 Welsh constituencies - 16,047.

Victory for the Gelli residents who had campaigned for years against the Nant-y-gwyddon landfill site came with a National Assembly report which was highly critical of the former Rhondda Borough Council for allowing the tip to be established. All tipping, both domestic and industrial, was stopped and some 120 local people were later offered compensation.

Once again there were problems on the Rhigos mountain road which was closed for six months after a landslip caused by subsidence blocked it. Repairs cost some £450,000 but at the other end of the valley, the National Assembly announced a relief road for the Rhondda Fach at Porth.

Rhondda was still maintaining its prominent sporting profile. This year the highly successful women's basketball team, the Rhondda Rebels based at the Rhondda

Fach Sports Centre in Tylorstown, won the British National Championship, taking the title out of England for the first time. The Rebels had already won the National Cup and so completed a fine double.

The new Rhondda was clearly not as male dominated as the old Rhondda for not far away from the Rebels' home, the valleys' first girls soccer team, the Ferndale Fillies, was founded.

2002 The Rhondda now stood to benefit from Objective One money, finance from the European Union for the poorer parts of Britain among which are the South Wales valleys - areas too dependent on part-time, low paid, low skilled jobs and where incomes are less than 75% of the European average.

With drugs-related deaths on the increase local people showed their determination to tackle this major social problem persisting among some young people in the valleys by forming RAID - Rhondda Against Illegal Drugs - another example of robust local initiative.

The valleys' musical traditions continued to be maintained as the Cory Band won the British Open Championship while the major award at the first annual Pop Factory Music Awards went to the Manic Street Preachers.

2003 In the second election for the National Assembly for Wales, Plaid Cymru were not able to repeat their success of 1999 and Geraint Davies lost his seat to Labour's Leighton Andrews.

Penygraig Rugby Club found itself making unwelcome newspaper headlines with allegations of performance-enhancing drugs being taken by squad members involved in the Silver Ball cup final against Pontypridd in May. Disciplinary action was taken against them and the club secretary by the Welsh Rugby Union.

At the gateway to the valleys at Porth, £1.3 million of Objective One money was made available for opening a training centre and 'learning cafe', Porth Plaza, on the reclaimed site of the former Cymmer Colliery as efforts to shape a new Rhondda were maintained.

Proposals for an eight turbine wind farm on the hilltops between the two Rhondda valleys were mooted and raised the possibility of the valleys once again becoming a source of energy in a way quite unimaginable to the Rhondda's old miners. Some 200 years after the first hesitant attempts to tap local natural resources, the valleys' potential wind power could begin writing another chapter in the Rhondda's eventful industrial story.

APPENDIX

Rhondda mining tragedies with multiple deaths

(arranged in chronological order)
Deaths are caused by explosions unless otherwise stated.

October 6th 1836	Lower Dinas Colliery	4 killed
January 1st 1844	Middle Dinas Colliery	12 killed
December 3rd 1844	Dinas Fforest Level	6 killed
April 14th 1850	Middle Dinas Colliery	2 killed
July 15th 1856	New Cymmer Colliery, Porth	114 killed
March 18th 1857	Ynyshir Colliery (Jones's Navigation)	4 killed
May 10th 1857	Old Cymmer Collery	2 killed
May 23rd 1862	Ynysfeio Colliery, Treorchy	2 killed
February 17th 1865	Bute Merthyr Colliery, Treherbert	4 killed
July 21st 1866	Tylacoch Colliery, Treorchy	2 killed
November 8th 1867	Ferndale Colliery	178 killed
January 23rd 1868	Tylacoch Colliery	2 killed
June 10th 1869	Ferndale Colliery	53 killed
February 24th 1871	Pentre Colliery	38 killed
January 27th 1872	Bute Merthyr Colliery, Treherbert	2 killed (in a shaft accident)
December 6th 1875	Penygraig Colliery	2 killed
April 11th 1877	Tynewydd Colliery, Porth	5 killed (by flooding)
August 15th 1878	Dunraven (Tydraw) Colliery, Blaenrhondda	2 killed
January 13th 1879	Dinas Colliery	63 killed
December 19th 1880	Naval Colliery, Penygraig	101 killed
February 21st 1882	Parc Colliery, Cwmparc	4 killed
September 11th 1882	Coedcae Colliery, Trehafod	6 killed
February 1st 1883	Coedcae Colliery, Trehafod	5 killed
May 11th 1883	Crown Level, Treorchy	3 killed
August 21st 1883	Gelli Colliery	5 killed
January 27th 1884	Naval Steam Colliery, Penygraig	14 killed
December 24th 1885	Maerdy Colliery	81 killed
January 18th 1887	National Colliery (The Cwtch), Wattstown	39 killed
January 7th 1888	Ferndale Colliery	2 killed (in an underground haulage accident)
May 13th 1888	Aber Colliery, Porth	5 killed

October 12th 1889	Ynyshir Colliery	3 killed (by a roof fall)
September 9th 1895	Tynybedw Colliery (The Swamp), Pentre	6 killed (in a shaft accident)
January 28th 1896	Tylorstown Colliery	57 killed
November 12th 1900	Cambrian Colliery, Clydach Vale	4 killed (in an engine house explosion)
August 4th 1901	Dinas Level	4 killed
January 22nd 1903	Glamorgan Colliery (The Scotch), Llwynypia	2 killed (in a shaft accident)
March 10th 1905	Cambrian Colliery, Clydach	33 killed
July 7th 1905	National Colliery (The Cwtch), Wattstown	119 killed
October 30th 1905	Ferndale Colliery	2 killed
August 18th 1906	Penygraig Colliery	2 killed
August 27th 1909	Ely Colliery, Penygraig	7 killed (in a shaft accident)
March 11th 1910	Clydach Vale	5 children and one adult drowned when a colliery dam collapsed.
April 8th 1913	Tylorstown No. 8 Pit	3 killed (by a roof fall)
July 4th 1923	Tŷ Mawr Colliery, Trehafod	4 killed
August 9th 1931	Maerdy No. 2 (Locket's) Colliery	3 killed (in a shaft accident)
January 25th 1932	Glamorgan Colliery (The Scotch), Llwynypia	11 killed
June 9th 1937	Cymmer Colliery	3 killed
November 25th 1941	Blaenclydach Colliery (The Gorky)	7 killed (in a runaway tram)
January 10th 1952	National No. 9 Pit, Tylorstown	2 killed
November 22nd 1956	Lewis Merthyr Colliery, Trehafod	9 killed
June 4th 1959	National No. 9 Pit, Tylorstown	2 killed
June 17th 1965	Cambrian Colliery, Clydach Vale	31 killed
October 8th 1968	Maerdy Colliery	3 killed (by a rock fall)

BIBLIOGRAPHY

Rhondda Collieries	by David J. Carpenter (2000)
The Fed	by Hywel Francis and David Smith (1980)
Hymns and Arias	edited by Trevor Herbert and Peter Stead (2001)
Rhondda Past and Future	edited by Ken Hopkins (1975)
The South Wales Coalfield Directory	by Ray Lawrence (1998)
The Rhondda Valleys	by E.D. Lewis (1959)
South Wales Collieries: Volume One	by David Owen (2001)
Musical Rhondda	by Dean Powell (2000)
Welsh Coal Mines	by W. Gerwyn Thomas (1977)
Democratic Rhondda: Politics and Society, 1885-1951	by C. Williams (1996)
Valleys of Song	by Gareth Williams (1998)

INDEX

A

B

D

E

F

G

H

I

J

K

L

M

N

O

P

Q

R

T

Y

Z